P9-AGS-345

Stop People Pleasing:

Be Assertive, Stop Caring What Others Think, Beat Your Guilt, & Stop Being a Pushover

By Patrick King
Social Interaction Specialist and Conversation Coach
www.PatrickKingConsulting.com

Table of Contents

Chapter 1: The Fatal Need to Please

I once had a friend named Muriel. She worked at a large technology company. She was in a middle-management position, which large technology companies can't seem to get enough of.

Muriel was well-respected because she seemed to be selfless and often took the burden of the entire office on her shoulders. She gladly accepted any piece of work her manager had, even if there were other people who could take care of it. In fact, sometimes Muriel took jobs from supervisors other than her own. "Just trying to carry the load and help out," she'd say.

Muriel had a habit of going above and beyond the call of duty. She worked hard to accommodate as many people as she knew. She'd take over presentations that cohorts were stuck on. She stayed late at least two nights a week. Maybe twice a month she would go out for lunch and offer to bring back sandwiches for her entire unit. Most of the time, she didn't ask to be paid back.

Her thinking was that she had to make herself an invaluable asset to the organization. This was particularly important to Muriel because she was terrified of being unemployed—she'd spent 22 months on unemployment, during which she thought nobody would ever hire her again. She figured that by working extra hard, other people in the office would consider her indispensable and could never replace her.

But somewhere along the way, Muriel turned that obsession into subconscious obedience. Not only did she want to make everyone around her satisfied and happy, but she also became utterly petrified of rocking the boat in any way.

Muriel worked in the marketing department. Her job was to suggest and execute product packaging design elements that made her company's products look attractive. She'd studied art and graphic design in college and fully believed in the "less-is-more" principle—that you shouldn't overload a given product package with too much clutter, extraneous information, or bad imagery. The market trends overwhelmingly agreed with her, and so did the sales data.

Unfortunately, her managers *loved* all that stuff. They believed customers wanted to see every single piece of information they could possibly want right there on the box.

Muriel knew this wasn't true and wanted to say something about it. But she didn't. She was afraid of rocking the boat in any way. She couldn't lose her job. So she simply nodded in assent at design meetings and supported their decision to clutter the package of their new product with unappealing imagery, thorough but unreadable information, and a lousy-looking cartoon mascot rabbit that had nothing to do with the company or the product.

The product failed for more reasons than just the packaging, but it didn't help. Either way, Muriel thought she'd done and worked hard enough to merit her staying in her job, because she'd striven to make everyone happy.

But when layoffs started two months after the product died, Muriel was the first to be let go. She was mortified. She felt that she had done everything right and made herself irreplaceable to the company. When she asked why, the human resources department said she hadn't done enough to distinguish herself as a vital contributor to the company. She didn't seem to have any ideas to move the company forward and appeared to be content just to keep the office in order.

Muriel descended into full-on panic mode. What had happened was the exact opposite of what she believed: keep your head down, work hard, and you'll get properly rewarded. She wanted everyone she worked with to feel happy and supported, but she somehow got punished for it.

What was the cause of Muriel's downfall? She was focused on pleasing others and gaining their approval and put her actual job priorities second. She wasn't doing what she was hired to and was only acting to prevent feelings of rejection. In hindsight, it's no surprise what happened to her.

Muriel was, in short, a people-pleaser and a stark illustration of how self-defeating people-pleasing can be.

What Is People-Pleasing?

Generosity and friendliness are excellent qualities to possess. They help communication and cooperation between people. They're necessary in order for societies to get along. In almost every scenario, they beat the alternatives of selfishness and hostility. These are traits that are beaten into our heads from childhood for good reason.

But don't confuse people-pleasing as generosity and friendliness. They may appear identical from the outside, but what drives a generous person versus a people-pleaser couldn't be more different.

A people-pleaser is kind to a fault, as you can see from Muriel's example. The drive for their kindness is *not* that it's just the right way to be or that they want to enrich people's lives. Instead of coming from a sincere desire to make the world a better place, people-pleasing stems from insecurity, fear, and shame.

A people-pleaser is worried about rejection. They have a need, as we all do, to be accepted and treasured—to be loved. But in people-pleasers, this need is amplified to the extent that they will bend over backward just to not lose that love or acceptance. They are driven by avoiding negative consequences rather than creating positive possibilities. Additionally, they feel that they are always on the brink of rejection, so this urgency causes a type of panic that is characterized by doing anything possible. People-pleasing is a *defensive* act, whereas genuine concern and generosity are affirmative practices.

The people-pleaser at the same time also seeks approval, because approval is the sign that there has been no rejection. This is why they will jump through hoops for a simple smile and thank you. These elements taken together create someone who feels that they must always be serving others in order to be accepted. Some specific impulses are detailed below—how familiar do they sound to you?

People-pleasers are always cheerful in all situations—on the outside. A people-pleaser never complains about anything. They have no apparent negative feelings. They have a smile on their face every moment they're awake—at least when others are observing. They think they're doing so to make everyone around them feel happy when, in fact, their sunshiney behavior is probably making those people uneasy. They are more transparent than they realize, and being around someone who is obviously putting a false face on is off-putting and uncomfortable. At best, it seems dishonest; at worst, it's manipulative.

People-pleasers never assert what they think, believe, or want—even if they are unhappy. With people-pleasers, it's all about everyone else. If they're going out with someone, they'll never recommend what to do or where to go. They'll never speak up if they're having a terrible time. They don't want to ever be the reason for unhappiness or dissatisfaction. They'll simply agree with the general sentiment of the group rather than risk rejection or being an outcast. They feel, whether accurately or not, that they are fine with everything. This allows resentment to build little by little over time until they are a volcano waiting to erupt.

***People-pleasers promise to do everything for anyone*—even if they hate it or are lying.** People-pleasers are in the habit of offering the moon and stars to their friends. They'll pledge to do things their friends don't want to do or things they know will delight their friends and earn a reaction of "Thank you so much! You're the best!" But people-pleasers don't necessarily plan on actually *doing* these things; they just *say* they will with the intent to gain temporary approval and make their friends happy. In reality, their continued promises and inaction just tick their friends off, as it becomes apparent that they are willing to be dishonest and only say what people want to hear.

People-pleasers never ask for anything—even if they need it. The people-pleaser pretends to deny that their needs are important at all and will therefore never request anything from someone else. They want to be seen as providing and unselfish. And even if a people-pleaser *does* muster up the nerve to actually ask for something, they'll give the person they're asking a million different options or opportunities to tell them no. They want to minimize the chances of inconveniencing or annoying others in the slightest. While they are talking about how selfless they are, the people-pleaser will grumble about their needs not being met or being addressed.

So what drives the people-pleaser to these seemingly dishonest and passive-aggressive behaviors?

As mentioned, people-pleasers are driven by a deep and piercing fear of rejection. They fear being spurned or deserted by others, and that fear plays a far bigger part in their people-pleasing than real feelings of goodwill. If they give and give and give, they believe there's less of a chance that they'll be rejected or abandoned. They're not really doing what they do to improve someone else's life—they just want to feel more positive about *themselves.*

However, that doesn't mean all people-pleasers are secretly mean, horrible beasts that are only after their own needs. They *can* be sincerely considerate and nice. They *can* be truly concerned about the welfares of their family and friends. People-pleasers just don't know what's really compelling them to please everyone. And they're very confused and mystified as to why, after all their efforts, they feel bitter, annoyed, or sad.

Consider the following traits, emotions, or self-beliefs. If a few of them feel uncomfortably familiar to you, then you may be a people-pleaser.

- You can't say no.
- You say yes but actually mean no.
- You agree to something but then fume quietly to yourself.
- You agree to do something but get mad at whoever asked you to do it.
- You complain that too many of your friends and family take you for granted.
- You feel that your expressions of love aren't mutual or being properly returned.
- You feel unappreciated for all the things you're doing for others.
- You feel upset, hostile, misunderstood, or duped.

- You feel unwanted, unloved, unvalued, or disregarded.

- You worry about troubling or irritating other people.

- You feel fatigued or worn out with people you have a hard time saying no to.

- You feel guilty about doing something you want to do.

- You expect others to perceive why you're unhappy without you having to tell them. You then get angry when they don't.

- You try to be what others desire you to be.

- You don't offer your opinions and generally just go with someone else's.

- You can't reveal your emotions when they're different from those of friends or family.

- You back away from being upset.

- You have a difficult time standing up for yourself.
- You're not aggressive in doing what you need to do.
- You never say how you feel because you're afraid you'll cause unpleasantness.
- You just want everyone to be peaceful, live in harmony, and never have a problem with anyone or anything else ever again and maybe have a unicorn or leprechaun on the side. No problem, right?

What Causes People-Pleasing?

Habits rarely develop in a vacuum, and people-pleasing is no exception. There are plenty of possible root causes of people-pleasing, and childhood is often pointed to as the origin. But whoever it was, and whatever the circumstance, your tendencies toward people-pleasing are rooted in being disapproved of or rejected by someone from whom you seek validation. This could have been your parents, teachers, classmates, abusive partners, egotistical friends, or people who simply suck.

Those negative responses (especially if they came in the form of physical or emotional abuse) kept compounding and adding to your poor self-esteem. That's the power of continual rejection—you will do everything in your power to prevent it, and that often takes the form of pleasing others. The way you can prove worth to yourself and others is to be servile and try to accommodate everyone's wishes.

Childhood roots of people-pleasing. The most powerful and present influencers in any family—more than faith or cultural background—are the parents or guardians of the household. Parents are supposed to be the protectors, the forces that keep us from harm, damage, and despair. Children exchange seemingly *unconditional* love for their parents or, at the very least, depend on them for their security.

Our childhood experiences with parents or other family authority figures color our attitudes and behaviors that emerge when we've grown up. Psychologist Hap LeCrone, specifically addressing the problem of people-pleasing, confirmed, "The problem often comes from long-held feelings and beliefs of inadequacy going back to childhood and adolescence, when the people-pleaser's attempts to please parents or caregivers were rejected, made conditional or otherwise unobtainable."

As such, a child understandably seeks praise and affirmation from their mother, father, or guardian. Centuries of evolution have cemented this impulse in us—making our parents happy with us is a survival instinct.

But when a child does something to irritate or anger them, a parent or guardian might express disapproval, possibly through punishment. We then understand their love as *conditional*. If we don't behave how our parents want, we sense they're rejecting us. We may perceive them as being emotionally unavailable or at best only occasionally available.

If we feel disapproved over and over throughout our childhood, we take on that disfavor ourselves—it becomes how *we* think we are. We internalize that disapproval as *we are not enough and we are inadequate*. In turn, it wreaks havoc on our confidence and self-esteem. After all, if the main figures in your life said you were a duck, you'd probably believe you were a duck. It's the same with our sense of confidence and self-esteem—hearing a message often enough, especially during childhood, when the brain resembles more of a sponge, can be damaging far into adulthood.

Those messages shape how we view our other, adult relationships. We allow friends, employers, and significant others—not ourselves—decide how valuable we are.

We ignore our own needs and work overtime for them so they'll see us as valuable people they'd never think of rejecting. But the value we feel from this kind of behavior isn't real, and it's not something we can depend on over the long haul. You may enjoy seeing the barista from your local café, but take away his ability to make coffee, and what remains? Not much of an incentive to spend time with him.

Codependency. This is another common cause for people-pleasing. Codependency is when you are excessively dependent on someone else, whether it be your spouse, significant other, or friend. We desperately care for them and seek their approval. However, we may harness a belief that love is conditional, only given to us if we meet all of someone's demands and behave as they want. We may fear abandonment or rejection, and to compensate we try to get affection out of others by being good boys and girls. If we please someone over and over again, we figure they'd love and accept us for all that we do for them.

All these actions and behaviors are symptoms of codependency, and it directly feeds into why some of us are relentless people-pleasers. We fear letting them down and try everything we can to make them happy so they'll continue to like us. It's an understandable impulse—but it's also imbalanced and stressful.

Agreeing to never disagree. This is a cause of people-pleasing that can slowly grow over time. People-pleasers dare not say anything that jeopardizes our safety and security. We always let the other person choose where to eat, we never challenge their viewpoints if we disagree with them, and we just "go with their flow" to avoid disruption or disagreement. After all, any disagreement is an opportunity for rejection. Further, we never know how unpleasant the retaliation or confrontation might be, so we avoid it altogether.

Things we need or want become insignificant to whatever everybody else needs or wants. Instead of giving voice to our own concerns, we submit to those of others. Imagine a spouse whose partner has strong political convictions and goes out of their way to support and affirm them—even though their own views may be very different or even opposing. They're afraid that voicing their beliefs will cause an incurable rupture in their relationship. Very rarely is it an intentional act to mold someone's psyche in this way, yet the instinct to please is widespread and common.

Get over it? Some people—most likely those who are affecting us this way—might say all talk of problems we've had in the past (especially in childhood) is an excuse. "How long have you had to get over it? Why don't you just let this go?!" They probably won't get how ironic that insistence sounds since it's another form of rejection.

But to answer their question, not only can't you get over it quickly, but you also really don't have a choice. Repeated traumas and mistreatment especially have long-lasting effects that don't go away the minute they stop. In his book *The Divided Mind*, John Sarno explains, "Feelings experienced in the unconscious at any time in a person's life, including childhood, are permanent. Anger, hurt, emotional pain and sadness generated in childhood will stay with you all your life."

These deep-seeded issues always manifest in our relationships. We subconsciously find partners, friends, or associates who amplify our deepest traits *and* flaws. And we reenact our experience in some way in the context of those relationships. In the case of people-pleasers, we give other people the reins of power and immediately place ourselves as their subordinates. This isn't to say one can't learn to live and thrive with these memories or influences, but it's almost impossible to *forget* them—which seems to be what our unsympathetic friends insist we do. That's unrealistic.

The Spotlight Effect

Human beings tend to dwell under a certain illusion that we're being watched by everyone else. Living under the limitations of our own viewpoint, we tend to think everyone in our circle is looking at and judging how we look and behave. This is known as *the spotlight effect,* and it's an inflated sense of self that can cause several ill effects in our lives and relationships. We're afraid to go dancing because we think everyone will see what bad dancers we are.

The spotlight effect is a mental distortion that causes us to feel foolish and ashamed on a daily basis. We're positive everyone's looking and cataloging our every action and reaction and are quietly ridiculing, lamenting, or mocking us. This makes us over-modulate our behavior or even recede from the public altogether to avoid further perceived embarrassment.

But the spotlight effect is almost totally imaginary. For one thing, it's not "scalable." If everyone is preoccupied with their own needs and interests, then there's really no possible way they could be spending their energies on the twists and turns of another person's life. At most, maybe a couple of people are paying attention to most of your moves, and they're likely people you're already close to who are supposed to know you better than anyone else. And even they have their own matters to concentrate on.

Unless you're a public figure, a rock star, a social media star, or anyone else with high visibility, the eyes of the world are most likely not trained to study everything you do and say. Even if you *are* a public figure, your estimation of how much the world is watching you may be greatly distorted.

The spotlight effect can still be a problem, and it greatly worsens the plight of people-pleasers. They already feel concerned that they may fall short of others' expectations. But if they're also suffering from the spotlight effect, those feelings are amplified and multiplied because they believe their every move and mistake is being noted by everybody else. They're even more flustered and motivated to right every wrong, bend over backward, and avoid any slight hint of disapproval or rejection. Their concern turns into full-on panic. They feel if they don't fix a problem fast, they'll be spurned by an entire group.

To battle the spotlight effect, you need to take the big step outside yourself to gauge if other people really are taking notice of you. Concentrate on and observe other people's reactions to what you're doing. One thing this will do is give you a break from your own internal nervousness—that alone takes care of a significant part of the problem. It will also likely show you that far fewer people are focused on your every move than you think.

Why You Shouldn't Be a People-Pleaser

Being under a constant directive to please everyone you can impacts you and your emotional health in several adverse ways.

Self-neglect. When you're so consumed with the perceived needs of others, you're not paying yourself any attention. You could be overlooking or ignoring things you need to do to take care of yourself. This could include anything from exercise and stress management to paying bills and just having fun. Maybe you've made social plans after work with friends you haven't seen for a while, but you find yourself working long into the early evening to fix a problem that could have waited until the next workday. Or you find yourself skipping a workout to deal with a family issue that's not really an emergency for you.

These are not just mental or emotional problems: they can easily turn into physical health issues. You must be able to equalize your needs with those of other people and strike a fair balance between the two.

Suppression, resentment, and passive-aggression. Putting yourself in a subservient position to everyone else will naturally make you build up anger and bitterness with the people in your life. After spending so much time placating others, this resentment can leak out in the form of cutting remarks or scornful quips. Such passive-aggression is never beneficial to relationships and can cause severe damage over time.

A people-pleaser must always cultivate a spirit of giving and selflessness—which is going to stuff more difficult feelings like rage, anguish, and animosity deeper and deeper inside you. Make no mistake: if these negative emotions don't get acknowledged and addressed for a long period of time, they're going to come out in fierce, possibly violent ways. You could experience a total emotional and mental collapse and potentially a physical breakdown as well.

Consider a submissive spouse who spends too much time working on their partner's needs and has to shelve their plans and goals to do so. Over time the spouse might have to deal with a slow-burning anger over never being able to do what they really want, and after a few months of quiet simmering it all comes out in an unforeseen rage against their partner.

Inability to enjoy life. If you're always worried about everything you need to do for others, of course you'll be less able to take pleasure in anything life has to offer. How can you focus on your own happiness when you're so concerned about being responsible for the happiness of others? You'll be too mentally and physically exhausted to enjoy a good meal, a weekend road trip, or your child's Little League game.

And this could result in a *real* bit of the spotlight effect—your friends and relations will be able to read your dissatisfaction all over your face. This can have a huge effect on our children: what are you teaching your kids when you're merely showing up for them but appear completely detached and disconnected?

Stress and depression. The very definition of stress is having more requests and needs than you can manage. When you're trying to please everybody you meet, the number of demands on your time certainly grows with no end in sight. The stress of these unmet demands soon slides into full-on depression, and you get stuck in a cycle that's very difficult to escape. Your to-do list never gets shorter, and it keeps getting filled with things for *other* people.

When a people-pleaser is struggling to meet all the demands they imagine are placed upon them, the levels of stress go off the charts just from the amount of work they put themselves through. When they've exhausted themselves making life betters for others but haven't experienced any prosperity of their own, that can cause a deep depression that only stops when they start a new round of people-pleasing. That's how the cycle works.

Exploitation. If you become known as a people-pleaser, you're also opening yourself up to being taken advantage of. More people will think you're willing to do anything for them, and they may start piling on more requests than it's fair for you to handle. Selfish and exploitive people will capitalize on your weaknesses without a second thought. Even people who *aren't* so mean-spirited won't know when you're overburdened and will expect things from you that you simply can't deliver.

This is particularly acute in the workplace. For instance, a senior executive who's more concerned about profits might place an unreasonable amount of work on your plate that you execute without obvious complaint. Then one of your peers, who's a generally amiable sort, sees how effectively and loyally you complete all kinds of tasks and they start considering you the "go-to" person for all sorts of things. They have no idea you're being exploited and spending nights at the office, simply because you don't give off the impression you feel that way.

The need to control. The myth about people-pleasing is that it's an act of selflessness and sacrifice. But in reality, it's much more selfish. In trying to do everything for everybody, you're trying to manipulate other people's opinions, feelings, and reactions toward you from emotional debt. You're *really* trying to exert control over their lives and situations in a sneaky and underhanded way. At the root of it all, we please and serve because we want a certain outcome from people. We want there to be a wellspring of emotional debt that keeps us in people's good graces or orbit. You can imagine how this can easily turn manipulative. Over time this impulse develops into a need and you become a control freak.

I've seen this happen at family Thanksgiving dinners, where the cook in charge (traditionally, frankly, the mother) lords over every single duty in the kitchen, despite offers from other guests to help out in some way. The people-pleasing mother has done everything for everyone in such an intense fashion that she believes nobody else will get it right. So she does all the work, eats at the table with droopy eyes for ten minutes, and then goes straight back to work on the pumpkin pie and post-meal clean-up.

Nobody knows the "real" you. People-pleasers have an image to maintain, and that comes at a cost. You shield and conceal your feelings to the point that people don't know who you truly are. They only know your people-pleasing disguise. Your desire to be well-liked and cherished by everyone, ironically, will make you more alone and detached—and maybe inauthentic as well.

If the "real" you eventually comes out, it could be far uglier than you'd like. You might fear getting inebriated because you'd be more likely to reveal all your private thoughts and viewpoints, particularly disparaging comments about the people you've been trying to please all the time. Whereas if you were more honest and forthright before, your complaints could have been more diplomatically expressed (and maybe solved ahead of time).

People-pleasing is not the same as generosity or goodwill. It's not something you do because you have true interest in the betterment of humankind or concern for your loved ones. Rather, people-pleasing is a manifestation of unhealthy gaps in our emotional lives and the need to satisfy the ego. Being able to tell the difference between such counterfeit kindness and genuine compassion is easier than you might think, and found-out people-pleasers aren't regarded highly. More importantly, they don't regard *themselves* highly enough.

But even with all the solid arguments against people-pleasing, it's something we still do. To stop that, we need to figure out what forces are behind people-pleasing—where we get the belief that we need to do it. That's what we'll talk about in the next chapter.

Takeaways:

- The need to please others may appear to be generous and selfless, but it is one of the most selfish ways of behavior. People-pleasing is borne out of fear, insecurity, and a need for approval. It is predicated on the sad belief that you are not enough and that you thus need to increase your value by catering to people's needs and desires.

- The origins of people-pleasing instincts can come from a variety of sources, but the dynamic is always the same. You sought approval, were denied, and had to prove yourself in another way. You were gradually taught through experience that you received better outcomes when you served and placated people, so that became your natural state of being.

- This compulsion is further compounded by the spotlight effect, in which we have the distorted belief that everyone is constantly watching us and picking us apart. This is detrimental for "normal" people, but it's even worse for people-pleasers because it drives takes their insecurity to new levels, which causes a host of detrimental behaviors.

- Make no mistake about it; people-pleasing is harmful. You may get the approval you seek on a short-term basis, but it will be fleeting and fake. Then you will have to deal with the consequences—for instance, repression and suppression leaking out in passive-aggressive behavior, finally exploding like a volcano, or generally compromised happiness and health because of the overwhelming number of tasks you give yourself. Finally, you might end up with skewed relationships because you are putting yourself in a subordinate role and constantly putting on a face.

Chapter 2: The Origins and Causes of People-Pleasing

You see someone cut in line ahead of you. You know it's not right. You understand you're perfectly entitled to remind the person where the back of the line is. But the thought of speaking up causes a rising tension within you, tying your stomach in knots and forming a lump in your throat.

You can't bring yourself to do it. You decide that it's better to let the occasion slide without ruffling any feathers. With that decision, you feel the tension within you subside, your stomach relax, and your throat unclog. *Ah, that's better.*

If you're a people-pleaser or someone who constantly feels like you can't assert yourself, the sensations described above might be all too familiar. You feel them every time you want to say no to others' requests or have feelings and opinions that run counter to what people expect you to have or are faced with any situation that needs you to prioritize or assert yourself in some way.

But while you may be familiar with the scene that plays out during such occasions, how well do you know the behind the scenes of the script you're continually running? Have you considered peeking behind the curtain at the origins and causes of such tendencies to please others and refrain from asserting yourself? What might be the reasons you feel such overwhelming tensions and negative emotions whenever you're in a situation where you need to stand up for yourself, say no, and refuse others?

This chapter will be all about looking into those origins, causes, and reasons, the underlying mechanisms that continue to drive people-pleasing and nonassertive behaviors even when they're proving destructive to individuals. While popular psychology might simply pin down the origin of such behaviors to childhood traumas, the real story is a more complicated cornucopia of psychological insecurities, distorted beliefs, and irrational fears. They *might* involve childhood experiences but are typically ongoing thinking patterns shaped by the current environment or cultivated by the individual themselves.

Consider the case of Jackie. Growing up as the eldest of four siblings in a fatherless home, Jackie learned responsibility early in her life.

From a young age, she became very good at sensing what others need and want even though they don't say it, and she has made it her personal mission to see to it that those needs and wants are fulfilled. She helped her mother with house chores, worked while studying, and served as the second mother to her younger siblings. This pattern of behavior eventually permeated into her friendships, work relationships, and romantic attachments too. She took pride in being the first person everyone calls if they needed help, a stand-in, or just someone to listen to them.

She considered a lack of time for herself as somewhat of a badge of honor, an indication of her selflessness and devotion to everyone around her.

Now a 45-year-old mother of two, Jackie still staunchly lives by the belief that being a worthy wife, a reliable mother, and an overall good person means always putting others first. She holds a full-time job while also taking care of everything in the household, feeling shame every time she feels like needing help from her husband or kids when it comes to house chores.

She believes that, as the mother of the home, she's responsible for everything from keeping the grocery list updated to keeping everyone happy and contented. She feels guilty about taking any time for herself to exercise, get regular health checkups, have a good time with friends, or just unwind by herself, because she's aware of the ever-growing list of things to do and commitments she can't just blow off without seeming like an irresponsible person.

Eventually, Jackie begins to more frequently suffer from an assortment of physical ailments, from the common cold to migraines to stress ulcers. And even so, she feels guilty about getting sick—because then she's incapacitated from fulfilling her proclaimed purpose, which is to take care of others, instead of having to be taken care of.

For people like Jackie, the real problem isn't their people-pleasing behaviors. Such behaviors are merely the visible manifestations of deeper issues, like skin bruises that show up as a consequence of the tissue trauma beneath them. In other words, people-pleasing is a symptom rather than the cause.

Several causes may underlie people-pleasing behaviors. Four in particular tend to rear their heads repeatedly.

First, for some, there is the distorted belief that serving others is natural and that looking out for oneself comes last. Relationships are all about serving, and the more one-sided, the better. Over time, they may have generalized such a tendency to subordinate themselves to everyone else they meet in their lives. If you possess this belief, it's easy to see how extreme guilt would prevent you from doing otherwise.

Secondly, many people-pleasers suffer from self-worth issues. They feel a sense of self-worth and a chance for acceptance only if they say yes to everything asked of them.

Third, many of those who are eager to please equate pleasing people with kindness and being good. Conversely, they equate saying no and self-assertion with harshness and being bad. This mindset makes them vulnerable to being taken advantage of, as they do everything they can to preserve that image of always being "good."

And fourth, many people-pleasers behave the way they do because they fear confrontation. They would rather bite their tongue until they bleed than say anything to rock the boat, ultimately building a life of resentment and unexpressed emotions.

These four specific causes of the so-called disease to please are what this chapter is focused on discussing. If your personal and professional relationships have been infected by this disease, it's important for you to first understand its origins in the context of your own experience and your own psyche.

When you understand why you behave the way you do, you are in a better position to know how to free yourself of this people-pleasing tendency. You will know the mindsets you need to catch in yourself and change, as well as the specific solutions and actionable steps that will work best in your situation. So to better equip yourself in the next stages of kicking this self-destructive habit, first take some time to learn all about the following specific causes of people-pleasing.

The Need to Please and Serve

From the time you were a kid, you are likely to have been taught that being considerate of others is always more admirable than putting yourself first. You were praised for being generous enough to share that pack of cookies with your sibling or to give that other kid a chance to play on the swing after you've had some time on it. On the other hand, you were admonished every time you refused to share or stand aside for the sake of others.

While there are certainly important values ingrained in such teachings and experiences—for example, those of generosity and compassion—they are typically taught with such one-sided vigor that you're likely to have developed a distorted belief that you're never allowed to put yourself first.

You have grown to believe that you should always serve and put others first instead, to the point that doing things for yourself brings about intense feelings of guilt on your part. Never mind that such things are actually expected or even necessary for your personal well-being. You've simply been conditioned to think that doing those things for yourself is cause enough for scorn and self-reproach. You find yourself needing to please and serve others instead to avoid feeling the guilt that comes with prioritizing yourself.

If you have thus grown to believe that your purpose is to please others, you would naturally think that standing up for yourself and refusing others simply go against your core values. You expect yourself to uphold generosity and kindness by always pleasing others. So when you do upset or displease someone by prioritizing yourself, you feel immense guilt—guilt that you take as a sign that you've violated some significant moral code. You consider that huge guilt as a reminder that refusing others and prioritizing yourself must be bad and that you should therefore just stick to putting others first all the time.

For example, Dave is a hardworking, humble manager who's always ready to take the fall for any of his team members. He thinks that because he's a leader, everyone else on his team is his responsibility, even to the point that he would end up doing the tasks he delegated them if they failed to do so. He believes that he's expected to be the all-around person for every task and glitch and feels huge guilt if he fails to cater to the needs or solve the problems of his every member.

He doesn't confront any of his subordinates about poor output or even misbehaviors, because he fears that if he does so, they might feel bad, lose confidence, or turn against him. Instead, he doubles his own efforts just to cover for every mistake and please everyone on his team, even if it means sacrificing his personal or family time. Convinced that putting everyone else first is part of his duty as a leader, Dave is filled with guilt at the thought of taking any time to prioritize himself over his team members.

So in addition to feeling guilty about putting yourself first, the intense need to please and serve others also derives from a feeling of responsibility for others' emotions and reactions. If refusing to grant a favor causes a friend to feel bad or neglected, you feel that that's on you.

You feel answerable for every disheartened expression or disappointed look, because you believe you had the power to avert that if only you succumbed to what they wanted. And because you feel responsible for everyone else's happiness and mental health, you are willing to sacrifice your own just to save everyone else from feeling bad or troubled. You become overly eager to do whatever it takes to keep everyone happy, believing that such is a sign you're taking the best care of your relationships with others.

The problem with having this kind of mentality is that it reflects a skewed view of what healthy, satisfying relationships are all about. Healthy relationships involve a certain degree of give and take, a balance between considering others' needs, and seeing to it that you don't neglect your own. Serving others and wanting happiness for the people in your life are reasonably worthy desires—but not at the expense of your own health and happiness.

Insecurity and Feelings of Worthlessness

Another major cause of people-pleasing is a deep-seated sense of insecurity and worthlessness. When you have so many insecurities and think little of yourself, you feel that you should expect to be rejected anytime, and you often feel that you deserve it. You can't think of any reason for people to be interested in you, much less approve of you or love you.

Deep down, you're convinced that you're not enough as you are and that you're not worthy of love, and this leads you to always being on your guard for imminent rejection. You become overly sensitive to any cues that may signal such rejection, and that includes any frown or offhand remark of disappointment from people you try to refuse.

Such anticipation and fear of rejection drive you to people-pleasing, as you come to believe that you gain worth as a person only when you please or serve others as they wish. You have never believed that people can like you for you, and so you end up feeling the need to stretch yourself by pleasing or serving others in order to gain approval and love.

You do whatever it takes to avoid others' displeasure and rejection, because with your frail sense of self-worth, that rejection may very well equal the destruction of your very sense of self.

Take, for instance, Helen, a woman who spent her childhood and teenage years trying to win the approval and conditional love of a mother who doled out affection only when Helen showed obedient or submissive behavior. Now a wife and mother herself, Helen is still unconsciously repeating the same relationship pattern with the people in her life. She believes her husband is doing her a favor just by staying with her, and she fears that her children might discover she's not a good enough mother for them.

To compensate for her insecurity and feelings of worthlessness, she gives them all her time and service while disregarding her own needs. She considers herself worth their love only so far as they are pleased with how she behaves.

Feeling unworthy of love isn't something many people readily admit to. Sometimes it's even something completely unconscious, like an invisible but deep wound you don't know you have but still keeps hurting you enough to drive many of your behaviors—yes, including people-pleasing. Maybe you acknowledged it long before you even hit puberty. Or maybe you've managed to convince yourself you're no good compared to a sibling your parents have always favored over you or to your popular friend who always gets awarded all the stars.

You've come to see yourself as unworthy of acceptance and love, for why would people waste their time and emotional energy loving you when there are so many others better than you?

In your core, you believe that no, you're not worth any love freely and unconditionally given to you. But somewhere along the way, you've stumbled upon this idea: you may not be worthy of that love as you are, but maybe there is a way for you to win that love by always trying to be more, to give more, to serve more.

And so you've fallen into the habit of pleasing and serving others to the best of your ability in the hopes of gaining that love despite feeling unworthy of it. You see people-pleasing as the solution, the healing elixir for those deep wounds of insecurity and sense of worthlessness you've been nursing.

Equating People-Pleasing with Goodness and Self-Assertion with Badness

The importance of being a good person is often a central lesson taught at home and in school, right from the earliest days of molding a child. When you're a child, this is likely among the first pieces of advice mommy or daddy gave you: "Play nice," "Be kind," and "Be good."

Those three keywords are often used interchangeably, too—nice equals kind equals good, so much so that you come to think of this domain of behavior as black and white. You believe that you must always be nice in order to be a good person, and anything that taints such an image of niceness—for example, refusing to grant a favor or calling out someone for stepping on your rights—makes you a bad person.

There isn't necessarily guilt involved here, as with the need to serve others. This is merely a highly skewed perspective of how relationships should work.

Such a mentality of equating being nice with being a good person, and asserting oneself with being a bad person, is enough to produce people-pleasing behaviors in anyone. But those especially prone to being hardcore people-pleasers with respect to this cause are those who consider it very important that they are seen as good people by everyone, all the time. If it matters to you a lot that you are perceived by people as nice and good, you'll surely be ready to sacrifice inordinate amounts of time and effort catering to everyone's needs and wants.

You don't want a single person in your life unhappy about how you behaved, because it takes only one slip-up on your part to shatter that immaculate nice-person image you've been trying to protect. The result? Heights of people-pleasing behavior and non-assertion.

For example, Bob has always prided himself on being a nice person and a good friend. He feels that these qualities are what define him as a person and he does whatever it takes to live up to that image. Asked by a friend for a huge loan, he obliges even though he knows that his budget can't reasonably bear to do so. He believes that saying no makes him a bad friend and ultimately a bad person, and he doesn't want that.

So Bob does what it takes to avoid being that bad person and to remain a good friend. He lends his friend an amount he can't afford to lose. To offset that amount, he sidesteps several necessary expenditures for a couple of months, accumulating late fees and interest he now needs to pay off on his own. He suffers the consequences out of fear that refusing his friend's request makes him a bad person.

Wanting to be a good person and even wanting to be seen as someone who's nice are not dishonorable desires. But the idea that you can't assert yourself and at the same time be a good or nice person is a skewed notion. It's perfectly acceptable to be assertive as required by the situation, and it wouldn't make you any less of a good person for being so. In the same way, the idea that being selfless all the time necessarily makes you a good person is also a distorted view.

Selflessness, noble as it may appear, can become a vice if you indiscriminately use it not out of genuine concern for others but out of a need to project an image people can admire.

On the other side of the coin is selfishness, which despite its negative connotations is actually a concept worth relearning and practicing in regulated measures. Understood in a different light and applied under the right circumstances, selfishness can be good.

This good kind of selfishness is one that's necessary, a centering upon yourself in order to maintain your health and replenish your energy before you give of yourself to others and to prevent spreading yourself too thinly by catering to everyone else's demands. For the sake of your own health, happiness, and dreams, you need to practice this kind of selfishness without feeling guilty that you might be taking anything away from others. As a matter of fact, it's by allowing yourself to be selfish at times that you can ensure you'll be able to look out for others and share the happiness you feel for them more fully.

Fear of Confrontation

Finally, people-pleasing may also arise from a fear of confrontation. When you're afraid to rock the boat, you will be content with going along with what everyone else wants, feel pressured to accept every request, and never dare to say no or stand up for yourself. This composite of tendencies and behaviors give rise to a single pattern: people-pleasing.

Since you're perpetually afraid to be direct with people with regard to your own opinions, feelings, wants, and needs, you're likely to be reduced to becoming a pushover or a doormat. What's more, you may not always be aware that it is this fear of confrontation that leads you to behave in such ways.

While people-pleasing may thus be rooted in a fear of confrontation, that fear of confrontation may in turn be rooted in even more basic origins. You may be afraid to confront people with what you really want because you're afraid you might not be heard anyway. You may be anxious that trying to stand up for yourself may only find you humiliated in the end, should you fail to win that argument for your rights to be respected.

You may dread that confrontation might lead you to lose a job, a relationship, or your good reputation. You may be apprehensive that confrontation will force ugly, unmanageable emotions to arise—guilt, anger, and disgust, to name a few—both in yourself and in those you confront. The bottom line is that you're afraid that confrontation will only make things worse and that you won't be able to handle that either.

So to prevent things from getting worse, you have a solution—you avoid speaking up, saying no, or confronting anyone altogether and simply take what you believe is the path of least resistance. If it happens to be inaction, so be it. Your solution, in other words, is to become a people-pleaser.

For example, consider what you'll do in a workplace situation wherein you feel your ideas are always just quickly brushed aside and you're assigned the most menial of tasks despite having valuable skills and more years on the job than others on your team. You want to bring up your concern with your team manager, but you're afraid that confronting her about it would only make you look conceited or would lead her to think you're questioning her delegation skills and thus cause her to be angry at you. These fears about ruining your image and your relationship with your manager thus paralyze you from speaking up altogether and block any chance of improving your own job satisfaction and career growth.

One tricky thing about avoiding confrontation is that it doesn't necessarily mean you have no desire to confront anyone about your situation. A mismatch between what's demanded or expected of you and what you actually want to do often creates a desire for confrontation within you. However, because you're afraid of the possible consequences of acting on that desire to confront, you end up holding off on confrontation.

This often results in that desire for confrontation leaking out in other, usually ugly and damaging ways. Instead of being expressed directly, it brims over through indirect means in the form of passive-aggressive behaviors.

Passive-aggressive behaviors represent indirect, often unconscious expressions of hostility. You may not have directly said no to a colleague who's requested that you file a report on her behalf, but you conveniently forget to do that task as a way to indirectly express your resentment at having been asked to do so. Or you may assure your spouse that you're not at all mad he didn't call you once during his work trip, but you retaliate by acting cold and "forgetting" to update him about your whereabouts all week.

So while you have managed to stave off direct confrontation in an attempt to preserve goodwill in the relationship, your actions still end up backfiring by leaving you prone to passive-aggressive behaviors that undermine the relationship anyhow.

Thus, avoiding confrontation for fear that it might only make things worse ironically results in the very outcomes it's meant to deflect. The absence of confrontations doesn't mean your relationship is all healthy, and the presence of confrontations doesn't mean your relationship has gone to the dogs. In fact, the ability to rise above your fear of confrontation so you can handle conflict situations better is necessary to maintain healthy relationships.

No matter how compliant and adaptable you believe you are, you're bound to run into conflict at one point or another, simply by virtue of you being an individual with your own set of thoughts, feelings, needs, and values that may very well differ from that of others. If you are to keep your relationships with others (and with yourself) healthy, you'll thus need to have the ability to tolerate being in the face of conflict and get past your fear of confrontation.

People-pleasing can be a hard habit to kick, especially because it's not a blatantly nasty tendency to have. In fact, it often helps you appear supremely likable and noble and occasionally rewards you with feelings of contentment when people repay you by smiling and saying thank-you after every favor you grant and every transgression you let slide.

But when you look deeper into the causes and origins of why you're really bending over backward to please people, you will recognize just how nasty people-pleasing is, maybe not with respect to others but with respect to your own self. Sticking to people-pleasing is a sure sign that you continue to cultivate within you an intense need to serve others, insecurities and feelings of worthlessness, mistaken assumptions about what being a good person entails, or a restrictive fear of confrontation.

It's time to ask yourself whether you'd really want to keep living your life this way, chained to the self-destructive habit of being at everyone else's beck and call 24/7.

If your answer is no, then it's time to pull yourself up by your bootstraps. By understanding the causes of people-pleasing, you've already taken the first step to breaking free of its chains. Now it's time to take the next step forward by learning the ways you can stand up for yourself, say no, refuse others, and overall just stop the people-pleasing mania you've let run your life for one day too many—in other words, it's time to learn how you can get better at treating yourself better.

Takeaways:

- There are many causes of people-pleasing behavior, and they start with the beliefs we hold about ourselves in relation to others. Simply put, we are not the same; we are lower or inferior in some way. This sets up interpersonal dynamics that enable people-pleasing and in fact reward it. I've divided it into four main categories that cause these beliefs.
- First is a skewed definition of relationships and how serving others should be your first priority, to the detriment of yourself. If you possess this belief, you will be wracked with guilt if you attempt to act against it.
- Second is a sense of low self-worth. If you don't feel that you are equal to others or that others will accept you for you, then it becomes clear that your only

chance of acceptance is to bend over backward and serve people's whims.

- Third, we have been taught from infancy that generosity and kindness are admirable traits. Some of us take this too far and equate prioritizing oneself to be selfish and negative.
- Finally, many people-pleasers simply fear confrontation. They hate the tension and discomfort and will go to extreme lengths to avoid it. They don't want to make waves and are solely focused on flying under the radar.

Chapter 3: Reprogram Your Beliefs

The previous chapter discussed the beliefs that underlie people-pleasing behaviors—the belief that you live to please and serve others, that you're unworthy of love as you are, that asserting yourself means you're a bad person, and that confrontation should be avoided at all costs.

Clearly, people-pleasing arises from such distorted views of the world and of yourself. Instead of feeling like a whole person, enough and worthy as you are, you've allowed yourself to believe you're essentially lacking. You've come to need other people's approval to fill the gaping hole that a healthy self-esteem and self-love would have filled. Your skewed views and beliefs have thus negatively impacted the way you relate to others and to yourself.

Ridding yourself of the compulsive need to please people would thus require you to radically shift how you view the world and, more importantly, how you view yourself. This chapter is all about giving you the tools to do just that—change your behavior by reprogramming your core beliefs and perspectives, especially those that directly impact your tendency to please others first and place yourself last.

Changing Your Beliefs: General Principles

Changing your beliefs is no walk in the park. Beliefs, especially those related to people-pleasing behaviors, are often intertwined so intricately with your personal history, critical experiences, and general temperament that they tend to be melded with who you are. In a sense, you behave according to what you think, you think according to what you've experienced, and you become what you believe.

And because it's so hard to separate who you are from what you believe, a task like changing the entire flooring of your house might in fact be way easier than changing your beliefs. Hard labor is relatively easy to do because it's external to you, more concrete, and more controllable—and thus also requires less willpower and discipline on your part. But changing your beliefs? That poses a more difficult challenge. Trying to change what you think about the world and about yourself requires you to deal with something internal, abstract, and fluid, not to mention needing a high level of self-awareness and enormous amounts of focus and devotion.

But though changing your beliefs is a difficult task, it is by no means impossible. You can learn the best practices to carry it out, and with enough dedication and consistency, you'll be able to reprogram your beliefs to create a better version of you.

One of the most-trusted and proven ways to change your beliefs is by using the principles of cognitive behavioral therapy (CBT). This method posits that you can change the way you behave by changing the way you think. Basically, through CBT you learn to be more aware of the kinds of thoughts you have, hone your ability to differentiate between distorted and realistic thoughts, and work to replace your distorted thoughts with realistic ones.

The BLUE model is a specific CBT strategy developed by PracticeWise to help counter negative thinking. BLUE is an acronym that stands for the kind of extremely negative thoughts you should recognize in yourself when they do pop into your head. "B" stands for blaming myself, "L" is looking for bad news, "U" means unhappy guessing, and "E" represents exaggeratedly negative thoughts. Below is an explanation of each of these thoughts and how they manifest in people-pleasers in particular.

Blaming myself. There is a difference between being accountable for your actions and wallowing in excessive self-blame. This point is all about detecting when you've fallen to the trap of the latter. Extreme self-blame begins to breed in your mind when you start thinking *"It's all my fault"* or *"I've absolutely messed everything up."* While taking responsibility is a mature and commendable act, unduly blaming yourself for every bad thing that happens is simply counterproductive and has even been linked to mental health problems such as depression.

In the context of people-pleasing, you're likely to have thoughts of excessive self-blame after a half-hearted attempt at putting yourself first. When you refuse your sister's request to babysit for her, you may start to feel guilty when she begins to talk about how much trouble it would be for her to find a babysitter. You think that it's definitely your fault she would have to go through all that trouble if you decline. So you oblige, because you feel the weight of blame for things not going as smoothly if you did otherwise.

Looking for bad news. It's a common tendency to focus on the negative rather than on the positive. If you've just been given nine compliments and one negative comment about your presentation at work, chances are you'll be dwelling on that single criticism and beating yourself up for it. Be wary of thoughts that look for the bad news in every situation, because such thoughts are sure to distort your outlook for the worse.

In people-pleasing, such thoughts may manifest as a focus on the negative consequences of standing up for yourself. When you refuse a friend's party invitation, your mind zeroes in on the thought that refusing might cause your friend to harbor ill feelings toward you. You deemphasize all the positives of that refusal, such as getting your work done and getting to rest, because your mind has latched on to that single negative consequence of upsetting your friend. And so you end up prioritizing what your friend wants instead of putting yourself first in that situation.

Unhappy guessing. This points to the thought that things are going to turn out bad in the future. Even though there is no way you can know what will happen, you predict the worst outcomes. The anxiety and panic that such a thought then rouses can rattle you enough to turn your prediction into a self-fulfilling prophecy. If you have an all-important test to ace but you keep telling yourself "*It's going to be a disaster*" and fret about it so much you can no longer think straight, then you're playing right into disaster's hands.

Exaggeratedly negative. There are thoughts that completely color everything black, and you should be on the lookout for those. They may sound something like "*Everything about this trip sucks*" or "*Nothing ever goes right in my life*." Exaggeratedly negative thoughts suck out all hope and bring only regret and fear, making it all that much harder for you to start moving toward more productive ends.

If you're a chronic people-pleaser, you may tend to have exaggeratedly negative thoughts about yourself. You think that nothing about you is likable, so you push yourself to serve and please others in an attempt to make them like you. Take for instance Kylie, who's grown up believing "*I'm good for nothing and no one will ever love me as I am.*" Given that, she always spreads herself too thin just to please others and gain from them the love and acceptance she's never given herself. She thinks that refusing others will only prove to them just how useless and unworthy of love she truly is. Thus, she lives her life aiming only to please everyone else around her.

Recognizing when BLUE thoughts occur in your mind is only the first step toward changing them. The next step is to replace those BLUE thoughts with true thoughts. While BLUE thoughts are biased toward negativity and catastrophe, true thoughts are more positive and realistic. True thoughts help you have a fairer perspective and guide you toward taking positive actions instead of just wallowing in self-pity and defeat.

Say you have a BLUE thought that goes, "*If I skip this PTA meeting so I could have my migraine checked first, it means I'm a bad parent.*" First, you need to recognize that such a thought is exaggeratedly negative and needs to be replaced with a more realistic true thought. To think up a true thought, Amy Morin suggests asking what you would say to a friend who presented you with such a dilemma. Would you tell your friend that missing the meeting would mean they're a bad parent? Probably not.

Instead, you would probably tell them, "*It's better to have your migraine checked first, because you can't be a good parent if you end up becoming too sick to care for your family. Missing one meeting wouldn't mean you're a bad parent. Besides, you wouldn't be able to be fully present at that meeting with a migraine anyway.*" Now think those thoughts for yourself as you wish your friend would for themselves. Practicing that will steer you away from self-destructive people-pleasing behaviors and toward a healthier relationship with yourself and others.

Changing BLUE thoughts into true thoughts is a core process in reprogramming the beliefs that underlie people-pleasing. As discussed in the previous chapter, there are four primary beliefs: (1) the belief that you live only to please and serve others, (2) the belief that you're unworthy of love as you are, (3) the belief that asserting yourself means you're a bad person, and (4) the belief that it's always better to just go along with others. This chapter will elaborate on the true thoughts that should replace those distorted beliefs.

On the Belief That You Need to Please and Serve Others

BLUE thoughts: B—"I deserve to be blamed if I fail to put others first," L—"Not helping them now will negate all other times I did agree to help," U—"If I refuse them, they will definitely hate me and it will ruin our

relationship for good," and E—"Being selfish will ruin everything."
True thought: "It's okay and sometimes necessary to be selfish."

Being selfish is always bad. Such a notion, often drilled into our thinking since childhood, is one of the cornerstones that lead to a lifetime of people-pleasing behaviors. When as an obedient child you're taught that putting yourself first is tantamount to being a bad person, you develop a pattern of thinking that compels you to always put others first instead.

Something as simple as a playdate may have planted such seeds of thought in you early on. That tug of war for your favorite toy with another kid may have ended with your mother telling you to let it go and learn how to share, because that's what good children do. Doing as you were told, you were then praised for being kind. Discovering such rewards for putting others first, you thus keep on with people-pleasing in order to gain approval and love.

On the other side of the coin is what happens when you go against that fundamental lesson and instead decide to prioritize yourself. As a child, you may have tested such boundaries when you refused to give up your favorite toy for someone else. While adamant to assert yourself, you may have been guilted into giving it up anyway by a number of techniques: being told how sad you're making the other kid feel or being labeled a bad child, among others. From this, you learn that putting yourself first should rightly make you feel guilty. Eventually, as an adult you feel that something's not quite right about putting yourself first, even when it comes to such things as prioritizing your health.

So what started out as an innocent maxim—"Don't be selfish"—often becomes your undoing as it evolves into the self-destructive philosophy that putting yourself first makes you a bad person. Feeling guilt for prioritizing yourself, along with gaining approval for putting others first, becomes the fuel for the people-pleasing habits you find so hard to break.

To break free from your people-pleasing patterns, therefore, you'll need to reframe the way you think about being selfish. Being selfish here simply means focusing on yourself and putting yourself first, *not* necessarily at the expense of anyone else. It's about being attuned to your own needs and wants and valuing yourself enough to honor them instead of being quick to wave them aside in the name of pleasing others. Being selfish isn't always bad. In fact, it's necessary to be selfish every so often, for the following reasons.

You can't fully serve others if you're not 100% yourself. It's alright to want to serve others and to nurture the relationships in your life by being there for people when they need you. But in everything, moderation is key—yes, even when it comes to something as noble as service and dependability. There is a point at which putting others first becomes harmful, not just for you but for everyone involved.

See, what many people-pleasers fail to see is that sacrificing so much of themselves in pursuit of serving everyone else around them is sabotaging their very capacity to continue being there for others when it truly matters.

When you're constantly exhausted and frazzled, lacking sleep, and overloaded with stress from taking care of everyone else, sooner or later you'll get sick, demotivated, or simply indifferent about work, friends, and family. Not taking the time to sleep, eat, and rest enough is bound to take a toll on you, eventually robbing you of your capacity to serve others with genuine concern and pleasure. In an odd conundrum, being too selfless makes you unable to effectively serve those you want to please.

For example, Sandra is a tireless mother and a dedicated business executive. Wanting to be a selfless family woman and at the same time a career woman, she sacrifices sleep, often skips meals, and forgoes exercise and recreation so she could have more time catering to the needs of everyone in her family and workplace. Over the years, she develops severe stress ulcers from her unhealthy lifestyle patterns and finds herself confined to a hospital bed for surgery and required bedrest. In her zeal to serve everyone else around her, she eventually finds herself unfit to do much for anyone at all.

The interesting paradox is that in order to truly put others first and give yourself in meaningful ways, you have to know how to put yourself first and be a little selfish where it counts. By making time for yourself and taking care of your own health first, you are putting yourself in the best position to continue being there for the people around you when they most need it. So by being selfish, you claw your sense of self back slowly, and you can use this newfound energy to be better at whatever you choose to spend it on. Hopefully you choose yourself, but even if you want to choose others, you'll be better off if you are operating at 100%.

You're the only one responsible for your own self. Being selfish is necessary because when it comes down to it, you're the only one who can truly take care of you. Others may be able to remind you to eat well or even serve you food or urge you to exercise or take you to the doctor when you're not feeling well, but these are all external actions. It's only you who can consume that healthy plate of food for your body, gather up the self-discipline to consistently exercise, and pick up on your bodily signals that say when you need to go see a doctor. If you keep disregarding all these just so you could cater to everybody else, then you're putting your very survival at risk.

Remember, no one else will be able to do those things for you. Moreover, no one will care like you because they simply aren't you and affected in a tangible way. We'd like to think that our parents or siblings will come through for us when we need it, and they might, but they still won't be able to devote all of their time and effort to you. Only you can do those for yourself, so you have to do them without feeling guilty about it. People-pleasing has to take a back seat to self-preservation. In the end, self-preservation is our underlying goal, but it's easy to forget that on a day-to-day basis.

Being selfish does not equate to being irresponsible or disregarding everyone else. Just because you set aside housework for half a day over the weekend for some rest doesn't mean you're a lazy person. Just because you missed your friend's party doesn't mean you've turned your back on them forever. There is a difference between limiting the time you spend for others so you could take care of yourself and being an uncaring, insensitive person.

Give yourself permission to refuse others and miss a few social commitments here and there, if that's what you need to recharge your personal batteries. The world doesn't operate in black and white, and you consequently can't view selfishness as 100% negative. It's far from it. The typical stigma involved with the term "selfish" makes it appear to be a harmful act, and thus we are usually conditioned to avoid it.

There is a wrong way to be selfish: one that involves being driven by egotism and looking only to use others for personal gain. Such selfishness is indeed destructive rather than helpful. But it's rather the exception to the rule and not at all what we are talking about here.

We just want to take care of ourselves, put ourselves first as appropriate, and protect ourselves without necessarily inflicting harm on others. All we are encouraging here is to prioritize your needs occasionally and certainly ahead of the mere desires of others. This kind of selfishness is what will help save you from the destructive patterns of people-pleasing you have let yourself suffer. In addition to the above points on how to reframe your thoughts about selfishness, there are two main ways to proactively be selfish (in the good way).

Prioritize your body. Being a people-pleaser takes its toll on your physical health. If you juggle multiple responsibilities at home and at work and try to keep up with everyone's demands on you, you're bound to lose sleep, not have enough time or energy for exercise, and rely on food options served up fast but greasy and definitely unhealthy. Keeping with this pattern is guaranteed to make you more vulnerable to catching diseases from the common cold to serious heart disease. This is the way being a relentless people-pleaser can literally kill you.

So before you contract any irreversible damage on your body, you owe it to yourself to put your own health first. In fact, make that part of your new filter when you come to the crossroads of asking whether to prioritize yourself or others. Is this going to harm or be detrimental to your body in some way? Is it going to cause you to neglect it and overall become less healthy? If so, that should be a hard pass from you. It's a useful metric that will definitely prevent you from bending over backward for people if it would, for instance, interfere with your gym routine or sleep schedule.

Learn how to say no to demands so that you can make time for yourself to prepare and consume healthful meals, get enough sleep and rest, and engage in regular exercise. Block out time in your daily schedule for such essential self-care activities and protect those time blocks from being impinged on by extraneous social demands. These blocks of time belong to you and no one else. Get comfortable with telling people you can't take on a task or go to that gathering because you need to be at the gym or go food shopping or simply rest. It's necessary to be selfish in this way, because when your physical health is on the line, everything else hangs in the balance.

Prioritize your mind. With modern life presenting its own set of stresses at just about every turn, the meaning of self-care has evolved to place more and more emphasis on caring not just for your bodily fitness, but for your mental health as well. This is your other filter in evaluating whether or not you should do something—does it put your mental well-being in a state of unhappiness, tension, or discomfort?

Say your friend is throwing a big party over the weekend and wants you to come. Knowing your friend, you're well aware that the party is bound to be rowdy, loud, and crowded—none of which you enjoy. Realizing you're not likely to have a good time there anyway, the best thing to do for your own mental health is to politely but firmly decline the invitation. You need to see that rejecting the invite is not the same as rejecting your friend and that prioritizing your own peace of mind by just settling into a restful weekend is totally okay.

People-pleasers in particular are vulnerable to being in a constant state of psychological torment. They are often plagued by insecurities, feelings of worthlessness, excessive anxiety and guilt when refusing others, unrealistic expectations on themselves, and distorted notions about what being a good person entails. On top of all that, they may feel guilty about the very idea of taking care of themselves, whether physically or mentally. Save for the last part about guilt, if serving someone else brings up those negative emotions in you, it should be a pass from you.

Learn how to be your own best friend and respect your own needs and wants. Train your mind to pick up on self-defeating and damaging thoughts telling you you're not worthy of love and acceptance unless you do exactly what others want. Then avoid those actions, people, and impulses. The people who truly love and accept you will do so unconditionally. They will not reject you or withdraw their affection just because you refused their request or asserted yourself.

Most importantly, stop feeling ashamed and guilty about putting yourself first. Being selfish enough to take good care of both your mind and body is an essential life skill to master. On the other hand, people-pleasing is a toxic, damaging habit to have. Which of the two you nurture in yourself is up to you.

On the Belief That You're Unworthy of Love and Acceptance

BLUE thoughts: B—"I'm never enough and it's all my fault that no one likes me," L—"It doesn't matter that I have some positive qualities. My moodiness is enough to drive people away," U—"No one will ever love and accept me unless I do what they want," and E—"I'm the worst person anyone can be with."
True thought: "I'm worthy of love and acceptance just as I am."

Feeling insecure and unworthy of love is yet another driving force behind people-pleasing behaviors. When you feel inherently lacking, you try to fill that vacancy with approval gained from others. You always put others first, because you believe that's the only way to gain worth, esteem, and love from the people around you. You believe you're only worth something for so long as you are of use to others and that if you cease to please them, you lose value as a person.

So how do you reprogram such skewed beliefs? The key is to see yourself in a new light. You need to be able to realize your inherent worth as a person, recognize your strengths, and know that you don't need to be perfect for you to be worthy. In so doing, you'll be able to accept and love yourself first, instead of depending on others to do it for you. By building more confidence and focusing on your own priorities, you'll become approval-independent and stop using people-pleasing behaviors to feel loved and worthy.

The journey toward accepting yourself just as you are is especially challenging. To help you through, learn to apply the following principles for accepting yourself, as suggested by Paul Dalton.

You live the feeling of your thinking. How you experience the world, as well as how you feel about yourself, depends on what you think. If you think that the world will accept you only if you put others first, then you will see nothing but evidence of that. If you think that the only way you'll be happy is if others approve of you, then you'll feel the need to seek out others' approval and feel unhappy if they disapprove of you.

Take for instance Sarah, who thinks the only way to be happy is to gain everyone's approval. Every time she puts others first, she receives so much appreciation and love from them and that makes her so happy. If she fails to please others and gains disapproval instead, she feels unhappy. However, what makes Sarah unhappy isn't the fact that some people disapproved of her—rather, it's her belief that she can never be happy unless everyone approves of her. Her mistaken belief that happiness comes from outside of her is what's truly messing it up for her.

But while it's easier to spot the flaw in Sarah's thinking when presented that way, it's harder to notice such distorted beliefs in yourself. One way to help yourself spot such distortions is by asking yourself some hard questions about your beliefs and thoughts on relationships, happiness, and yourself. Ask yourself, *"What are the things I do to be happy?"* or *"What are the core beliefs I have about my worth as a person?"* Take it as an exercise of self-awareness and write your answers down in a journal so you can clarify your thoughts better.

Everything good is inside. In this modern age when social media has made it so much easier to flaunt status symbols and compare your life with others, it's very easy to believe that everything worth having is outside of you—awards and recognition, financial success, material possessions. This line of thought feeds what Dalton calls the "learned self," a version of you that relies on everything outside of you to feel worthy and acceptable.

However, what the learned self actually does is separate you from who you truly are and from that other version of you called the "unconditioned self." The unconditioned self is the authentic you, the innocent core untouched by all the criticism and trauma you may have been through. This self is the one that knows it is enough and worthy, even without all the trappings of external approval and material success. It is aware that everything good is inside and that true happiness can be found only within oneself. It's this unconditioned self that you need to revive so that you stop seeking others' approval in an attempt to feel worthy.

One way to revive your unconditioned self is to take a break, unplug, and have some alone time. Go somewhere peaceful and relaxing, where you can be free to reconnect with the deeper parts of who you are. Take this time to rediscover who you were before you allowed yourself to be pressured by society to turn into someone you're not just to please the world.

Your relationship with yourself determines your relationship with everything else. Your relationship with yourself impacts everything else in your life. If you have a negative relationship with yourself—blaming, berating, and seeing the worst in yourself all the time—then you'll be desperate to seek from others the acceptance and love you crave but cannot give yourself. The danger of this is that you'll be vulnerable to abusive and toxic relationships with those who take advantage of your desperate need for approval.

For example, if you think so low of yourself and believe you're unworthy of love, you may be more likely to tolerate even maltreatment from a partner. You may feel you deserve the verbal or emotional abuse you're enduring, because for so many years you've treated yourself in the same harsh way as well. You'll simply want to continue pleasing even those who are already taking advantage of you, because that's how you derive a sense of worth and love.

To get unstuck in that destructive pattern, start treating yourself with more compassion and kindness. Try to be a good friend to yourself. Instead of being the first to blame yourself for every mistake or disapproval from others, be gentle with yourself. Remember that you're allowed to mess up, that you're not responsible for others' happiness, and, most importantly, that you're allowed to put yourself first. As you learn to forgive and love yourself first, you'll also start to feel less of a need to seek out approval and love from others. You'll realize that while pleasing others may feel good for a moment, loving yourself feels even better in a lasting way.

Another exercise you can do to build your self-esteem is to make two lists, one of your strengths and one of your achievements. For example, in your list of strengths you may include such attributes as "creative," "focused," "good communicator," "resilient," and "honest." In your list of achievements, you might enumerate such things as "awarded best project," "successfully managed a team to achieve year-end goals," and "organized an art exhibit for charity." Having such lists makes it clear to you the talents, skills, and positive qualities you do have but often overlook as you struggle with your insecurities.

If you're finding it difficult to come up with things to put on those lists, try to get the help of a supportive friend or relative. It's understandably difficult to identify your positive qualities if you never feel worthy in the first place, so having another pair of eyes to perceive your qualities more objectively would really help. Keep those lists accessible and read through them every morning to remind yourself of what you bring to the table, whether or not people approve of you.

Finally, you might want to consider how your own expectations might be creating your insecurities and feelings of worthlessness. If you expect yourself to be the perfect parent, child, sibling, friend, neighbor, and colleague all rolled into one, never upsetting anybody or messing up any of those relationships, then you're setting yourself up for failure. You'll be bound to feel like you're never enough, because the reality is that no single person can be everything to everyone.

If you want to stop feeling unworthy and lacking, you'll need to readjust the standards you have set for yourself to make them more realistic. Make a list of the roles you play in life (e.g., father, friend, colleague) and write the corresponding expectations you have for each. Replace perfectionistic with more realistic expectations about what you can and should do for others as you fulfill each role. That way, you'll get to feel a sense of satisfaction as you meet those expectations instead of spreading yourself too thin trying to reach the impossible standards of pleasing everyone.

On the Belief That Self-Assertion Is Bad

BLUE thoughts: B—"I've wrecked everything by speaking up for myself," L—"Being assertive is no good; it only brings unwanted tension in the group," U—"If I stand up for myself, I'll ruin my relationships with others," and E—"Asserting myself makes me a bad person." True thought: "I can assert myself and still be a nice/good person at the same time."

People-pleasing may also result from the belief that asserting yourself automatically makes you a bad person, the kind that aggressively imposes their needs and wants on others. Not wanting to be seen as that bad, aggressive person, you thus go along with what others want and never stand up for yourself. You believe that asserting yourself means having to be aggressive in imposing your own needs and wants on others, and you don't want to be that kind of person.

Here's the problem with such thinking: the belief that the only alternative to being a people-pleasing doormat is to be an aggressive jerk is mistaken. You'll need to reprogram that belief by reexamining what being assertive really means. Assertiveness is about being able to speak your mind and stand up for yourself when the situation calls for it. It's about being self-assured and confident without being aggressive or arrogant. Being assertive doesn't make you a bad person; in fact, assertiveness is good. It's a quality necessary for you to nurture productive and satisfying relationships with others.

It's important to realize that assertiveness is not aggressiveness. While aggressiveness is likely to worsen a situation by its use of unnecessary force, assertiveness can bring clarity and resolution to a tricky situation. For example, if you feel you've been given an unfair performance rating by your supervisor, making strong accusations about favoritism is aggressiveness. The assertive way of dealing with such a situation is by tactfully expressing your concern and asking your supervisor to review with you the bases of the rating you received. Done appropriately, assertiveness results not in the ruin of your relationships, but in their improvement.

Understandably, assertiveness is not an easy thing to practice for people-pleasers in particular. If you're a people-pleaser, you're likely to be naturally caring and compassionate toward others, qualities that you may believe to be incompatible with being assertive. However, being assertive doesn't have to mean you stop being caring and kind. Through what Sherrie M. Vavrichek calls compassionate assertiveness, you can stand up for yourself in a kind and caring manner. Here are some guidelines Sherrie suggests on how to practice compassionate assertiveness.

Be guided by the golden rule. "Do unto others as you would want others to do unto you"—so goes the maxim. When it comes to having compassion while being assertive, this rule should be your guide. If you asked someone to do you a favor and they actually don't want to do it, wouldn't you rather they express it'd be too much trouble rather than do the favor while harboring resentment against you? You would probably prefer that they be direct with refusing you but that they do so in a gentle and tactful manner.

The same goes for when the situation is flipped. If doing someone a favor would be too much trouble for you, that someone would likely appreciate it more if you gently yet clearly expressed your refusal. They wouldn't want you doing that favor for them while gritting your teeth as you silently resent them. You may think you're protecting your relationship by trying to please them despite yourself, but by refusing to assert yourself you're actually straining the relationship by allowing resentment and ill will to breed. The best thing you can do for yourself, the other person, and the relationship is therefore to be assertive.

Aim for a win-win solution. People-pleasers are often tormented by a conflict between the needs and wants of others versus those of themselves. If you aim to please others, you tend to disregard your own needs and instead prioritize the needs of others, which eventually becomes a self-destructive pattern. To counter this, learn to assert yourself with the aim of arriving at a solution that respects the needs of both you and the other party. Acknowledge the valid concerns of the other person without disregarding your own needs. Better yet, offer suggestions that would help the other person out.

For example, if a coworker asks if you would cover a shift for him but you've already made other plans, you may respond with "*I understand you really need someone to cover your shift, but I'm afraid I'd be unavailable due to a prior commitment. Shall I check with Sam if he'd be up for it?*" Such response is assertive yet still helpful and supportive of a friend in need.

So as the above strategies have shown, you can be assertive while at the same time be a nice, compassionate, good person. You don't have to hold your tongue and do just what pleases others all the time for you to be considered a good person. Learn to think differently about what assertiveness means and how to practice it in daily life, and you'll soon start to replace people-pleasing patterns with self-assured actions that help you put yourself first when needed.

On the Belief That It's Always Better to Just Go Along with Others

BLUE thoughts: B—"I'm to blame if I can't find a way to be okay with what they want," L—"The negative consequences of rocking the boat are too severe to risk doing it at all," U—"Refusing or disagreeing with others will only spark conflict I cannot

handle," and E—"I have no choice but to please others because I'll never get over my fear of confrontation."
True thought: "I can learn to handle conflict and confront others in appropriate ways."

One of the hallmarks of people-pleasing is the inability to say no to others, voice out your opinions and emotions, and assert what you want. If you want to please everyone around you, chances are you tend to simply go along with what others prefer and never stand up for yourself. Even if you aren't interested in pleasing people, you might be pushed into it indirectly through a crippling fear of confrontation.

You're afraid to ruffle anybody's feathers, so you keep mum instead of speaking up. You don't want to rock the boat, so you comply with whatever demands or requests everybody else has for you. Fears of conflict and confrontation are strong motivators of people-pleasing behaviors, so if you want to stop being the quintessential doormat, you'll need to learn how to overcome these fears.

One way of overcoming your fears of conflict and confrontation is through a technique known as exposure therapy and the use of what is known as a fear hierarchy.

What is exposure therapy? Exposure therapy is the process of deliberately placing yourself in situations that cause you fear and anxiety. You'll need to immerse yourself in your feared situations in a gradual and progressive manner, starting from situations that cause the least anxiety and later advancing to those that cause the most intense feelings of fear. This technique allows you to practice staying with those uncomfortable feelings of fear and anxiety until they no longer bother you as much and you get to a point when you eventually overcome them.

Exposure therapy is useful for helping people manage a wide variety of fears and phobias. For example, it's traditionally used to help people conquer phobias of certain animals (e.g., snakes, dogs, spiders) or situations (e.g., heights, elevators, crowded places). To help people-pleasers in particular, exposure therapy is focused on extinguishing the fear of confrontation that prevents them from refusing others and standing up for themselves. Though it's typically conducted by therapists, you may also utilize the principles of exposure therapy and practice it on your own to help you get past your fear of confrontation and consequently diminish your people-pleasing tendencies.

To practice exposure therapy, you will have to immerse yourself in situations of conflict and confrontation. And since it's often difficult to come by such situations if you leave it to chance alone, you'll need to create those conflicts yourself. But before you start imagining that this technique will have you picking a fight with the first person you see on the streets, keep in mind that exposure training involves carefully selected, reasonable tasks paced gradually and in a progressive manner. For people deathly afraid of conflict, anything that involves assertion will help. This means that you're going to be working up a fear hierarchy, from mild conflict situations that trigger the least anxiety in you to more challenging confrontations that cause you the most fear.

Creating your fear hierarchy. The fear hierarchy is an ordered list of situations that elicit your fears and anxieties. It's something you construct that's made up of triggers and scenarios particular to your own experience and arranged in the way you deem fit.

For example, your list may start with the least anxiety-eliciting task of taking a longer time than usual to do something, such as taking your time paying and counting your change at the sales counter before moving aside for the next customer. Though not a blatantly direct confrontation, it creates a mild conflict situation between you and the next customer or the cashier. Though unlikely to spark a prolonged verbal clash, the situation will challenge you to stay with the rising tension you feel from taking more time than is reasonable to do something.

Eventually, you may work your way up to actually asserting yourself in a conflict situation, such as confronting a bully. This is bound to involve an actual verbal confrontation between you and another person, one who isn't likely to be the most forthcoming of people to confront. This will create an even higher level of tension and conflict for you to endure and is intended to be something you should attempt toward the end of your exposures.

Note that the fear hierarchy is intended to be a graduated list, starting with the easiest tasks and working up to the most difficult. It wouldn't be advisable or effective to start with taking a long time paying at the counter the first day and the next day be confronting a bully. You'll need to work through a series of steps with advancing levels of difficulty so that you get to gradually increase your tolerance of the discomfort that comes from being in conflict situations. Below is a sample fear hierarchy with specific confrontational scenarios you may work through in progressive order, from the least to the most anxiety-inducing. When you feel comfortable with the tension in each, as well as internalize the feeling that you can do these things without any ill-effects on yourself or the world, you can move to the next step. Keep in mind this is just a sample.

1. Take a long time remembering the passcode for your credit card as you pay at the counter.
2. Have a salesclerk differentiate two similar product models for you and take a long time hesitating over which to buy.
3. Decline an offer by a salesperson to try a product or upgrade a service.
4. Say no to a coworker asking you to cover for their shift.
5. Send food back in a restaurant.
6. At a party, inform the host that a snack was too salty.
7. In a restaurant, drop cutlery on purpose several times and request a replacement every time.
8. Let a friend know that you need them to return a thing that they

borrowed. State a specific date on which you want it returned.

9. Deliberately arrive late for a meeting.
10. Speak up when you disagree with a coworker's idea or plan.
11. Negotiate with an accounts representative to waive the late fees you were charged because of a system glitch.
12. Ask your raucous apartment neighbors to keep their noise down.
13. Dispute the results of a performance review your supervisor conducted on you.
14. Speak with a friend about their fault-finding patterns and ask them to stop being negative all the time.
15. Tell your boss to stop humiliating you in front of people at work.

Remember to tailor your fear hierarchy with respect to your personal anxieties and fears, which may vary from the above either in kind, in order, or in both. Construct your list specific to the confrontation scenarios with the most significance to you. Or if you find the above list mirroring the conflict situations you'd like to try out, you may rearrange them according to the intensity of fear they create in you. Also note that as genuine conflict situations are understandably not always possible to recreate in real life, you have the option of visualizing the scenarios instead. However, it's still best to actually experience such situations in real life whenever you can.

How exposure therapy works. The working principle behind exposure therapy is that when you force yourself to stay in the conflict situation and fully experience the range of emotions you feel in that moment—be it discomfort, anger, anxiety, or fear—you'll come to find those difficult emotions easier and easier to tolerate and accept. You can only manage conflict successfully if you've reached a point where you're comfortable enough to stay with the difficult emotions it may elicit, and that can only happen when you stop evading it every time it crops up. In essence, you find that things are not as bad as you thought they were, and you survived just fine. This allows fears and anxieties to slowly die down through the realization that negative consequences won't follow.

For instance, exposing yourself to the situations listed in the sample fear hierarchy above will have you experience the uncomfortable feelings and fearful thoughts that come with being immersed in conflict. Taking a long time to remember the passcode for your credit card as the line of customers waiting to pay lengthens will cause you to feel anxious, embarrassed, and tense. But as you continue to stay with those feelings and refuse to buckle to the pressure of moving along already, you soon discover that no matter how many pairs of eyes keep piercing at you, the world will not end and you will not die by virtue of that.

The most that can probably happen is that someone will tell you to hurry up, and that's about it. The same principle applies for every step of the process—you can say no, express disagreement, and speak up against wrongful treatment without it being the end of life as you know it. From such experiences, you learn that you can stay in a conflict situation and survive it. As you gradually expose yourself to more and more challenging scenarios, you also build a higher and higher tolerance for the discomfort that comes with facing conflict and confrontation.

Another thing you can try is to engage in relaxation methods while you're in the process of exposing yourself to conflict situations. As you feel your heart starting to race, your palms getting cold and sweaty, and your breathing becoming fast and shallow, you may counter those anxiety signals by doing some deep breathing. Consciously pace your breathing to be deeper and slower, taking five counts for inhaling through your nose and another five counts for exhaling through your pursed mouth. Deliberately relaxing your breathing will clash with the anxiety symptoms the conflict situation is eliciting. This will then condition your body and mind into thinking that you're actually not as anxious as you've let yourself believe.

What exposure training aims to make you realize is that conflict and confrontation aren't as bad as you have let yourself believe them to be. Saying no to a friend's invitation to a party won't lead to the catastrophic demise of your relationship or diminish your friend's goodwill for you. Telling a salesperson you don't want to subscribe to what they're offering won't kill you. Through exposure therapy, you get to see that you can confront people or even create conflict and yet you can still get through the situation unscathed. The idea this technique plants in you is that it's okay to confront others when the situation calls for it. You will likely never be free of that feeling of uncomfortable tension you'll experience directly after telling someone no, but it becomes easier and easier with more practice.

By learning how to overcome your fears of conflict and confrontation, you're equipping yourself with a valuable tool for banishing your people-pleasing behaviors. When you're no longer as afraid of telling people you think differently, of saying no to demands, or of standing up for yourself, you're less vulnerable to being a pushover. You learn to speak up and do what's best for yourself and to start making choices that protect your well-being and enrich your life. You stop being someone enslaved by the need to keep all of your relationships constantly enticing and satisfying for others. And more than just kicking the people-pleasing habit, you get the greater reward of becoming a person of your own.

Takeaways:

- A lifetime of people-pleasing will lead to some deeply ingrained beliefs that require reprogramming. A staple of changing beliefs is cognitive behavioral therapy, which is, in short, a way to combat skewed beliefs with thoughtfulness and pointing out negative patterns. The easy way to think about this is through BLUE—"B" stands for blaming myself, "L" is looking for bad news, "U" means unhappy guessing, and "E" represents exaggeratedly negative thoughts. We can apply these to the four major causes of people-pleasing behavior from the previous chapter.

- You must be more selfish. Often, we have the belief that selfishness is always bad and never good. The reality is that you must be selfish, even if you want to serve others, because only then can you operate at full capacity. Selfishness does not mean throwing others under the bus, and it simply means prioritizing your body and mind.
- You must accept and love yourself. Your relationship with yourself determines your relationship with everyone else, so you should be more compassionate to yourself and understand that acceptance is a choice—typically made more difficult by impossible standards and expectations you place on yourself.
- You must believe that assertiveness is not inherently bad and does not equal aggressiveness. Consider what you would do in other people's shoes and be creative in finding ways that both people win in a situation.
- You must accept and grow more comfortable with confrontation. A good

method to get over a fear of confrontation is to use exposure therapy. Specifically, create a fear hierarchy for yourself as related to confrontation. This will help you grow used to the tension and also show that you nothing ill will occur if you face your fears.

Chapter 4: Change Your Habits

Being a constant people-pleaser, as we've just discussed, can disrupt your belief system by undercutting your self-esteem, causing feelings of guilt, making you evade conflict, and weakening your confidence. These poor feelings feed into the creation of bad habits. Habits are automatic responses to what comes in front of us, and many of us at this point are just conditioned to automatically please and serve. In this chapter we'll investigate what those are and how to change them.

Janelle absolutely hated her job. She felt like everyone around her was a sycophant who only cared about their own cliques and social lives instead of the work they were supposed to oversee. The culture was toxic and there was a revolving door in terms of hiring and quitting. But she stayed at her company for eight years.

Why? It was all Janelle was used to. She didn't have time to question what was happening and assumed a lot of responsibility. If she didn't keep everyone's plates spinning, the company would (she thought) buckle under and go bankrupt, which would have been worse. Her days started to blur together, and she started to just go through the motions to whatever would get her home the quickest each night.

Janelle never expressed her opinions on how to improve the culture at work—she just assumed there was a process in place that was impossible to change. In her first job out of college at a law office, she learned the hard way that some types don't like to have their decisions questioned, thanks to a very angry criminal attorney who dressed her down. That memory remained with her for a very long time and kept her from making waves.

But finally, after eight years of feeling suffocated and silenced, Janelle had had enough. She left the company. She'd reached a point where there was no reason to hold back and explained in detail why she thought the culture was broken, what parts of daily operations needed to be addressed, and how they had to change to survive.

Janelle is a classic illustration of how easy it is to fall into bad habits, especially if there was some emotional basis that began it. She got into the habit of letting things slide and not bringing up her issues to the extent that she spent eight years in virtual misery. Are people-pleasers destined to this fate? Not if we take a hard look at our automatic responses and change our habits.

Becoming Self-Aware

The first habit we must develop is the habit of self-awareness. We don't understand *why* we people-please, and we're not aware *when* we're doing it. Lacking knowledge in these two phases means that we are doomed to repeat history. When we understand what causes us to engage in it, we can avoid those triggers, and when we understand how it feels when we're doing it, we can mitigate the consequences.

This begins with questioning the motives for your actions: "Why exactly am I going out of my way for this person?" "Do I genuinely care for them, or am I just afraid of what might happen without them?" "Would I be doing this out of free will, or am I doing it for someone else?" Try to come to terms with the emotions your people-pleasing behaviors are associated with—is there admiration and connection from you, or is there fear or guilt? Gaining self-awareness can be as simple as running through a checklist of questions anytime you feel that you are in risk of engaging in people-pleasing, designed to discover whether you are acting out of your own free will or a tendency to please.

Everybody struggles with viewing their emotions from an unbiased, objective standpoint. Especially as a people-pleaser, when you're placing someone else's interests and emotions above your own, it can be hard to give your feelings the proper respect they deserve. You're stowing your emotions in the trunk, after all. That's why it's important, as difficult as it is, to become aware when you're about to do it.

Acknowledging our own truths is how we learn to change ourselves. Otherwise, we'll just keep on reacting to feelings we're not really in touch with or aware of, and there's no way to control our personal realities in that case.

Self-awareness will help you understand why you're working so hard to gratify other people—if you're doing so because you really want to or because you think you *have* to. You'll understand if you're actually making things better or inadvertently making them worse. And before you lapse into an act of people-pleasing, you may well see an opportunity to make a different choice.

When you're about to do something with someone else that you're not sure you want to do, take note of the moment you're starting to feel internal resistance. When that happens, stop everything and question why you're doing it. Keep asking why until you hit the truth about yourself that you need to acknowledge. Alternatively, you can use the popular "five whys" method, in which you ask yourself "why" five times and answer yourself to get to the real issue you're having.

Let's say you go camping a lot with a group of friends. You generally take on most of the set-up chores, like pitching the tent, organizing the meals, getting the random supplies in order, all that stuff. You're the go-to person and you try to make other people happy in the campground.

Here's the thing: you don't actually *like* camping—certainly not enough to do it four weeks out of the summer. Everybody else seems to be having more fun than you are. All things considered, you'd really prefer to be in an actual house with a glass of wine and a nice Netflix binge session.

"Why am I camping?" Well, your friends like to do it, and you want to be sociable with them.

"Why does it always have to be camping?" Because you haven't offered up an alternative idea for recreation.

"Why do I do the lion's share of the setup when I don't even want to be doing this?" Because you haven't verbalized your need for help, you think it's easier to just do something rather than discuss it, you think you're the only one who can do it, and so on.

And you can keep going from there. Eventually, you'll hit a point that exposes the root of your problem, and hopefully this profound moment will make you reevaluate and change how you deal with people-pleasing.

Building Autonomy

The second habit to cultivate is the habit of personal autonomy. The thing with people-pleasing is that it takes your personal identity out of the picture. You operate under the power of somebody else's authority. You rely on the beliefs and thoughts of others. You dare not speak your opinions unless you know everyone else feels the same way you do. For all intents and purposes, you cease to exist. It sounds harsh, but it's an accurate description of someone who makes themselves subordinate to everyone else. There is simply no autonomy, and it is both a habit and a choice.

All of us need validation from others. We thrive on acclaim, compliments, praise, and overall kindness. There's nothing wrong with that. But people-pleasers rely *solely* on the approval of outsiders. Their low self-value makes them entirely dependent on other people's opinions. They are like a shadow, as they are completely reactionary to other people.

Why is this harmful? Because, again, it's a false bond. You think you're being accepted as part of a team or alliance, but in actuality you're becoming more isolated. Even if you're being complimented for what you've done, that reflects an action and not you.

You're fueled by your need for approval—not by your own character, qualities, or abilities.

That's why autonomy—the ability to think and act independently of others—is so critical. An autonomous person knows what they truly believe and why they believe it. They act freely and with self-assurance. They are able to effect changes themselves and don't shirk from their own responsibility. They insert their own opinions and don't falter when challenged. Of course, the belief that you can stand on your own is antithetical to thriving on approval from others. But it's this simple belief that enables autonomy to break free of other people's expectations.

When an autonomous person *does* help somebody else, it's because they feel real concern for someone or something based on their own emotions or principles, not those of the outside world. It's a free choice not born of a desire to avoid negative consequences of rejection or judgment. Autonomous people generate *real* respect from others—not just the passing praise or idle compliments that drive people-pleasers.

For example, suppose you're collaborating with others on your company's annual report. You've been put in charge of putting the written narrative together. You've noticed in the past that the writing in the report tends to be a little dry and uninvolving. You theorize that's why nobody really pays attention to them once they're published.

Other people who've worked on the report in the past few years think the writing's been fine. It says exactly what they intend to say, and there's no reason to put any extra effort into it than that. They don't see the need to "make people care" about what they present. They've told you not to work that hard—do it like it's always been done and move on.

You listen to their advice. Then you ignore it. You develop ways to present the data that makes it more understandable. You tell stories that explain your company's values. You write prose that's engaging but never off-point—things that nobody else had thought to do. The report comes out, it attracts attention from all quarters, the executives love the initiative you take, and someone thoughtfully gives you a new swivel chair in admiration.

Whereas before you would have gone the easiest route and done what was traditional, you've made a decision and moved forward based on what you knew was best, regardless of what others thought.

Now, autonomy is one of those things that is far easier said than done. But the difference in the above example is that you've valued your own opinion over that of others. Or you've at least valued it equally and not by habit put your own opinion as inferior to that of others. That's the first place to begin when developing the habit of autonomy. Whatever proverbial room you're in, you're there for a reason, and you should use that fact as evidence to support your independent thoughts.

Doing Less

A habit that requires doing less? That is a unique take.

In all relationships, whether personal or business, people-pleasers take the attitude that they have to do everything they can to the *nth* extreme for them to merely survive. This feeling results in their working overtime, above and beyond, to make them work. To them, there appears to be a linear relationship between the amount of pleasing they do with how much approval they receive. At the very least, a huge effort on their part is a necessary part of the equation.

Realistically, though, working too hard and doing too much don't make for a healthy union. If you're overworking in service to your relationship, then you don't have enough to function in other parts of your life. No doubt you mean well, but the imbalance takes away the relationship's strength and creates an unhealthy dynamic where the expectation of lopsidedness is enabled. It's wrong to think that one person doing excessive work in a relationship can make up for the *other* person's responsibilities as well. Simply stated, in that case, there isn't a relationship, at least not a sound one.

A great relationship, whether with your supervisor, friends, or significant other, succeeds because everyone in it takes responsibility for their own share of the effort. There is a sense of equity and consideration. Taking on other people's duties in addition to your own will only damage the relationship. The cliché is true: you can't really respect or love anyone else if you don't respect or love yourself—and that means knowing when you're working harder than you should and stepping back.

Fight the people-pleaser's impulse to make a lopsided relationship in which one person does all the work and doesn't get anything back. Again, this involves becoming self-aware. Examine your relationship from an objective point of view and understand if there's a disparity in how much each partner is doing. This will probably be easy to observe if you ask yourself and honestly answer the following question: "Would this person do for me what I did for them?"

When you've come to that awareness, stop overworking by simply *stopping*. At a certain point, there will have to be a line that you do not cross. This will never be comfortable, especially with our urges to do as much as possible to "ensure" our places in people's hearts. In fact, we feel that when we are not in motion, things are being forgotten and opportunities squandered. But consider the saying "less is more" and realize that stepping back will allow other people to step up and equalize the relationship. You must give people the space to act for you, not just react to you.

Let's say you're in charge of a family budget. This involves knowing what your family needs and how much to allot for it, balancing it out with the bills, rent or mortgage, and everything else a household spends for. Nobody else in your family really pays attention to the budget, because they just assume you have it all under control, which is a fair assumption if you don't say anything otherwise.

You do all the grocery shopping. You run all the errands. You administer everybody's phone plan and Wi-Fi access. You make decisions on what everybody's computer or technology needs are and spend accordingly. But you're exhausted from trying to sort out everyone's financial needs, and a couple of your kids are complaining that you didn't get the kind of drinks they wanted or that their connection's too slow for online gaming.

"Forget it," you think. "I can't make all these decisions anymore. If people need something, they're going to have to make a few of the decisions on their own. And it certainly wouldn't hurt if they did some of the shopping themselves." You make a decision to do less.

So you tell the kids to make lists of what they need or want. They have to figure it out on their own. You tell your partner you'd like them to actually do some of the shopping, especially for things that pertain to what *they* want. You have everyone monitor their own data usage on their phones. And when you have to be out of the house to shop, you have them take up a household chore that you'd otherwise do.

Was that so difficult, other than realizing that it needed to be done?

You've lightened your load, redistributed your duties, made others take responsibility for their own needs, and gotten yourself out of the people-pleasing circuit. Doing less and delegating and/or relaxing is a hard habit to embrace because, again, it feels like things are slipping through our fingers. They aren't. Inaction by you does not mean things are not being taken care of by others.

Learning to Let Go

It's an unkind fact of life that some people do and say terrible things. The unfortunate people who suffer from their actions and words can be haunted by them for extended periods of time, even eternally. Bullies and negative people have existed forever, and many never get the comeuppance they probably deserve. Some are even revered for the destructive way they are.

There's no need for us to sympathize or even try to understand those negative people. They don't matter; they're in the past. But many times, what they've done to us maintains a very active presence in our psyches. We can't let go of the awful emotions their callous actions and low opinions have instilled in us. We still allow what they put us through to restrict us in the present, dictate our thoughts, and keep us from striving to realize our possibilities. Whatever past experience has eroded your self-worth and self-esteem or made you fearful of negative consequences, attempt to recognize that it doesn't represent your life today. Your feelings aren't reality, and neither are your memories.

(Before I continue, I should make it very clear that people who have suffered through emotional, physical, and sexual abuse are not who I'm talking about here. Victims of those situations can't "just get over it." I don't seek to mitigate their pain whatsoever.)

It's easier said than done, of course, to put those painful memories away. You can't un-hear negative words. Deprogramming the junk they've put into you is not an easy process. Still, our staying stuck in the loop of the past is exactly what's holding us back.

We remember their criticism and hold on to it. Consequently, we live in fear of an invisible disapproval—which sends us scurrying to please everyone.

That's not really dealing with the problem. It's allowing the problem to control our thinking and stop us from growing. We are products of our pasts, but we are not our pasts, especially the parts that we did not choose. We are who we are *today*, and that is entirely a conscious choice.

Our first inclination when a problem arises is to try and get rid of it, but that doesn't necessarily mean *solving* it. We don't want to cope with the emotional distress the problem will cause, and we want to avoid all the painful ramifications that might emerge from it. But we're not processing the problem—we're just trying to avoid and forget it. You know that's not going to make it go away.

So when a memory of a distant hurt from someone else rises up in us, we run in fear from it and do everything in our power to make the current situation *feel* okay. That leads us into people-pleasing behavior.

For example, say you have a roommate you tend to do everything for. It's not that they're lazy or irresponsible, but you always put yourself in the position of cooking for them, doing their laundry, running some of their errands for them, and so forth. They seem a little uncomfortable with this arrangement and offer to take some of the load off, but you keep on doing it.

Why? Because when you were a child you were teased by classmates for being slow, never getting anything right, or coming up short, and their bullying has left a mark on you to this day. So in order to counteract it, you've turned yourself into a servant.

Letting go of the past is how we make these situations bearable in a real way. But you have to make the conscious decision to do so. You also have to acknowledge the pain the past event caused—this is a crucial step—and don't try to circumvent or deny how it makes you feel. And as painful or unthinkable as it may be, you have to assert that you're not going to allow past bullies to victimize you in the present. They're gone, and you're still here. I won't say you absolutely *have* to forgive them—but I will say, in many cases, that's not a bad idea. Most of us are just doing the best we can with what we've got and don't intend to maliciously hurt everyone around us.

When you come to terms with this sordid past and gain the habit of letting it go, you'll find yourself more confident and freer to be yourself—and to get off the people-pleasing train.

Being More Honest

People-pleasing, as we've discussed, involves putting on a disguise. You're cloaking yourself in service to others. This involves a form of dishonesty in which you conceal your true feelings, thoughts, and opinions. You certainly don't mention if there's something you need from someone else, and repressing your emotions is almost never a good thing in the long term.

That's why it's important to get into the habit of expressing yourself honestly. The more you communicate where you stand, the more people will know where you're coming from (and what your limits are). After all, people can't read minds, and to expect others to know what you want is an impossible task. Explain what you need or want without ambiguity, with the conviction it's what you deserve. You can think of it as being less filtered or speaking your mind more directly. Whatever the case, it's clear that you currently aren't honest with the people around you regarding many things.

This may involve expressing an opinion that others might disagree with, and that could result in some mild strain or tension. You have to allow yourself to expect that uneasiness and learn to be okay with it.

For example, let's say you hang out with a group of friends on a daily basis. Generally, all you ever do is hang out at a bar and drink too much. You like being in their group, and drinking seems to form a big part of the group identity. But it's starting to take a toll on you, physically and mentally, and you might notice it's not really making the group relationship terribly strong. Still, you haven't said anything because you don't want to alienate their friendship.

But now it's gotten to the point where you have to cut back and refocus on your own priorities. So you message the group and tell them you have to cut back, that you're concerned and worried about yourself becoming chemically dependent, and that you need to focus on getting healthy. In fact, it would be great if they all could try a group activity sometime in the actual outdoors.

A primary motivation in people-pleasing is to feel approval from others. But here's the thing: you don't *need* someone else's approval to do what you want to do. If you're not planning on committing a crime, hurting another person, or doing something destructive, you have the right to do whatever you want. Rather than tell someone you intend to do something and ask them if it's okay, just say you're going to do it. And then do it.

It's typical for people-pleasers to feel or at least question whether they deserve the things they want. They've been putting everyone else's needs ahead of theirs and haven't been thinking about themselves, so how can they know if they really merit what they want?

Here's your universal answer to that question: *yes, you do*. Instead of getting into the cycle of wanting something and questioning whether you really deserve it, just focus on what you really need. You might not get what you want 100% of the time—but that's better than the 0% chance you'll have if you don't try.

This includes setting boundaries for yourself (which we'll go more deeply into in the next chapter). People-pleasers don't dare establish limits over which others may not cross. In the process, even those who don't even *want* to take advantage of you—and most people don't—might do so because they don't know what your limits are. Defining your boundaries with total clarity goes a long way toward stopping future conflicts and blunders. And it helps you reclaim the part of you that mindlessly pleasing other people takes away.

You may feel extremely apprehensive about making these kinds of requests. In that case, you may need to do a little more work to persuade *yourself* that you're entitled to do it. This is where writing things down is extremely handy.

Before you make your appeal, write down the reason for your request. Be detailed and open about it. Concentrate on your reasoning and comprehend it as much as possible—because when you make your request, they're going to be the main part of your negotiation strategy.

Obviously, if you're just asking someone to do you a favor, you don't need to whip out PowerPoint and create an intricate slideshow with charts and graphs. But even for relatively small asks, it's worth writing your thoughts down to putting them in order. And feel free to review what you've written down with someone else that you trust. If you're having a hard time coming up with solid reasons for this request, then it might not be reasonable to begin with.

Being Strong Under Pressure

Once you've decided to be more assertive, you *will* face disapproval—the sworn enemy of every people-pleaser who ever lived. This might involve some verbal criticism or loud disagreements. And some of them may sting, no doubt. But they won't kill you.

Facing this kind of reproach might be the hardest part of your journey out of people-pleasing behavior. But it's also the one that might pay off the most, because it will shore up your toughness in almost any kind of crisis, even situations deadlier than a spat.

The first thing you need to consider is the source of your criticism. Quite often, the real problem your critics have isn't about you at all—it's *them.* It's worth thinking carefully about whether their complaints are really intended to correct your "error." They may actually be verbalizing and projecting their own issues into their censuring you. Or they may have no idea what it's like to be in your situation or have the faintest clue about your circumstances. Constructive criticism is fine, but it's frequently clouded by the experience of someone other than you. The harder they push against you, the deeper the issue within them. Take that possibility into account.

If you're face to face with whoever's judging you, it's almost always worth *not* giving an immediate reply. When someone's hurling criticism at you or complaining about how you do something, take a few breaths to settle yourself down.

Also, consider that you do *not* have to respond at all. You're under no obligation to answer your critics' negativity if you don't want to. You can just dismiss them and go on your way. This isn't advisable in *every* case—you probably don't want to dismiss the opinions of your partner or a police officer—but it's certainly fine in disputes that really don't matter that much in the long run.

But if you choose to engage in the back and forth, remember what we just talked about in the last section: disagreements are okay. Two people not having the same viewpoint on a given issue is common. Frequently those two people go on to lead productive and fun lives after their disagreement.

I realize this is harder than I might make it sound, because everybody wants others to be on their side, because the alternative involves tension. But there's nothing wrong with simply being unable to come to an accord and accepting that impasse. There are too many people in your life to expect that they'll all fall in line with your beliefs and actions. Once you accept that, you'll probably feel a great burden lifted from your back.

In all situations, when you're dealing with someone who's angry with you, don't immediately assume that you're the one in the wrong. People-pleasers tend to accept that snap judgment to keep the peace, but it's not always correct. If you truly can't deal with the idea that someone might be disgruntled with you, then you're more liable to compromise your beliefs to put yourself back in their favor. In addition to *what* your critic is saying, try to figure out *why* they'd say it. The answer may say more about them than you.

People-pleasers also tend to be automatic assenters. When somebody asks them to do something, they do it—bam, right on, no questions asked. But it's best to resist that impulse to simply agree on the spot. That will cause some minor distress in the recovering people-pleaser, because denying an instant response will create an uncomfortable strain on their emotions. If you can resist caving in the first time you face pressure, it will never be more intense or difficult than that. You only need five seconds of extreme willpower to remain strong under pressure and not buckle. It just gets easier every time thereafter, especially with the same person.

But once again—*you are entitled to do what you want or need.* That includes delaying your response until you've had more time to consider the request, whether it's a few minutes or a couple of days. You're being completely fair in postponing your reply until after you've had a chance to think it over. Your priorities are the most important here.

Not Feeling Responsible for Other People's Feelings

Finally, get into the habit of understanding exactly what you are responsible for and what you are not responsible for.

The people-pleaser heaps a whole lot of responsibility on themselves—even in situations that don't necessarily involve them—to take care of other people, including safeguarding their emotions and how they feel. If we cause someone to feel badly because of our newfound assertiveness or sense of self, we feel responsible for their plight and act to prevent it.

You instinctively want to be someone's emotional guardian, and this desire to avoid creating unhappiness in others creates the same unhappiness in you.

So if someone exhibits a negative or sharp feeling due to you asserting yourself, the people-pleaser will immediately consider it their duty to change that feeling back or prevent it in the first place. As we know, this isn't a matter of generosity—it's a matter of gaining approval and removing insecurity. If you're doing this out of habit, you are unconsciously feeling that you are responsible for how someone feels and deals with emotions and how happy they are at the end of the day.

That isn't logical—any more than a child being responsible for their parents arguing or a spouse being responsible for their partner's work issues. But it happens a lot. Whatever the case, we spring into action to try to assuage our misplaced guilt.

You need to realistically look at whose feelings you're *actually* responsible for. It's impossible for you to carry so much responsibility for anyone other than yourself, and it's harmful to have that expectation. The idea that you do have that great responsibility is a creation of your own mind—it's not reality.

The world is in a constant state of flux, with a lot of moving parts and billions of people and animals operating them. You can't be responsible for everyone's feelings because there are too many elements for one person to handle.

Think about your own situation. Life is essentially nothing but a series of variables, many of which we don't control. When you make a decision, you generally consider several factors: what situation you've been presented, influence from those close to you, social engineering, and so forth. You depend on a multitude of conditions, circumstances, and drives to navigate your life. So does everybody else. You can't logically be accountable for all of it.

Instead, assume and assert your own *self*-responsibility—things that are completely under your control. These would be your thoughts, your words, your actions, and your feelings. Every person is responsible for their own emotions. And they are the *only* person responsible for their emotions. To a certain degree, you must grow the habit of being less empathetic to other people and more compassionate to yourself.

You might think that trying to make other people happy is virtuous or somehow makes you a better person. But it doesn't. Sacrificing your happiness and health to make other people happy is not noble. It's selfish. When you give someone who is constantly feeling sorry for themselves attention, you're training them to feel sorry for themselves. You're also training them to need you. Too many people get their sense of self from helping others who don't need their help. These people have no idea who they are, but they know that other people need them. That's what they tell themselves, at least.

People-pleasers are not born—they're made. They've been conditioned by the habits they have taken on and left unaddressed, because any letup in their constant efforts to make others happy could bring their house down. But just a few alterations in approach and thinking go a long way in eradicating bad habits, setting up good ones, and finally attaining emotional freedom.

Takeaways:

- Unfortunately, over time, please-pleasing behaviors tend to become solidified as habits—automatic responses to the world. We may intend something different, but if our first and second instincts are to please, we are not improving at being assertive. Therefore, it becomes necessary to change a few of these unconscious habits to break your detrimental patterns.

- Build self-awareness of why you are engaging in people-pleasing behaviors and you will be able to realize that you aren't doing it out of free will or generosity. This can be as easy as asking yourself "why" five times in a row to try to understand what's behind your actions.

- Build autonomy and become freer from the opinions and thoughts of others. Value your own opinions and thoughts, and don't automatically subordinate yourself to others.

- Do less and stop creating one-sided relationships. You've conditioned people to rely on you, and to reverse this, you must give them the space to act for themselves.

- Let go of your past. It informs who you are, but you are not your experiences and memories. Try to realize when you are acting out of the past or out of your own free will.

- Remain strong under pressure. When you stop people-pleasing, you will face some angry reactions. It's not necessarily their fault because you have conditioned their expectations. But this is where you must not fold under pressure, like you previously would have. It only takes five seconds of extreme willpower, and it gets easier every time thereafter.

- Stop taking responsibility for other people's emotions and happiness. Everyone is responsible for their own emotions and happiness. You do not need to be someone's emotional guardian, especially if it is harmful to you.

Chapter 5: Set Your Boundaries

Creating boundaries is essential in your efforts to stop people-pleasing. Many times, we're unaware that we're giving full access to others and letting them encroach our private space. When we let that happen, we risk losing ourselves and our identity, which contributes to our people-pleasing habit.

I've known Rhett and Grant since childhood. We were all part of the same social group in high school and went out together frequently until we went to different colleges after graduation. After about 10 years apart, they reconnected over the Internet, realized they lived pretty close to each other, and started getting together more.

At some point in those 10 years, Rhett started up with a multilevel marketing company. That's a business that sells a certain kind of product (usually) but also aggressively recruits other people to represent and sell its product—and also tries to recruit friends and family as well in hopes of getting bigger commissions.

Grant, as he told me, can't stand multilevel marketing companies. They all reminded him of pyramid schemes. His parents had a couple of friends who took part in those programs in the 1970s, and they were always being bugged by them (and wound up going broke).

Furthermore, Grant had a certain boundary that he was quite firm on: he didn't like his friends hard-selling him—whether it was products, politics, religion, or anything. Grant had heard (and done) enough "sales pitches" for work; he had no interest in suffering through ones given by his friends in their private time. He didn't want to mix business and friendship and also didn't want to feel preyed upon by supposed friends.

But of course, that's what Rhett did. He constantly tried to get Grant to become a representative for this company, kept pushing his buttons, and sent him refrigerator magnets and charts that Grant found completely meaningless. At one point, Rhett even sounded a little hostile about the fact that Grant wasn't interested.

Finally, Grant had to tell Rhett off: he had an issue about personal friends trying to sell him on certain things. Grant didn't want it in his life, and if Rhett was going to keep doing it, he'd have to stop having contact with him.

Rhett got pretty incensed at Grant and cut off all contact. Afterward, Grant said he felt a tinge of remorse, thinking he should try to salvage the friendship. But Grant bypassed that regret and decided to let it drop. He had to stick to his principles and deal with the consequences.

The relief was almost immediate. Grant felt that he'd stood up for his code—that friends shouldn't badger their friends into deals they don't want—and that as difficult as losing a friend was, it's far easier than being poisoned slowly.

Boundaries don't just apply to other people. We also have to impose some limits on our *own* behaviors and habits, because there's no way we can properly function without regulating our own activities. Examples of boundaries we set for ourselves include the following:

- limiting how much time you spend on a certain job
- keeping a budget so you don't overspend on things you don't really need
- watching how much you consume certain foods or beverages

- setting reasonable and realistic annual goals
- keeping a daily schedule that doesn't overload you with work or social responsibilities

You can't do it all for yourself, so how can you expect to do it all for everyone else as well? Self-discipline is a crucial part of living responsibly and happily, so it's always a good idea to start by defining your own personal limits. But it's important for a recovering people-pleaser to clearly establish boundaries with others.

What Are Boundaries?

In terms of human beings, a boundary is an invisible barrier that surrounds your personal space. This definition includes both physical space—the immediate, literal area around you—and emotional space. For purposes of our people-pleasing discussion, we're more interested in the emotional kind.

Boundaries set the limits of how much people can trespass into your emotional life. They regulate the "space" you need to be your true self with no duress, which you need other people to respect. This space is necessary for you to maintain a certain distance so you don't become too reliant on others or entangled with another identity. But a good boundary also defines who *can* get closer to you so you don't become entirely alone or aloof.

With sound boundaries, you feel freer to be yourself without the burden of others' expectations or demands. You have the room to be more creative, more free-flowing, more independent, and more unique. You get a nice buffer zone that allows you to think about certain situations more calmly and easily. At the same time, a reasonable boundary lets you invite who *you* to share your emotions with—after, of course, you've defined your own personal boundaries based on your needs.

People-pleasers either don't know about or drastically underestimate their need to establish boundaries, making sure others are happy before they're allowed to even think about finding their own happiness. So in seeking to stop the people-pleasing routine, putting your foot down and making clear boundaries is a step you can't overlook.

How to Tell It's Time to Set Boundaries

Especially when one's in the thrall of people-pleasing, it can be difficult to acknowledge when others are invading our personal space and overstepping our limits. After all, you've projected yourself as someone who's there for everyone all the time without any regard for your own necessities. For all intents and purposes, other people's obligations are inside your boundaries. If that's the case, then what is the point? So the first step in setting up healthy boundaries is understanding *when* that line is being crossed and what it *feels* like when it happens.

To do that, you have to pay attention to your body and mind. When you're around someone who's troubling you or wearing you out, how does your body react? Some typical symptoms might be a clenching of the gut or tension in your head. Also, explain what goes through your mind when you're around this person—is it confused, inattentive, or racing with ideas on how to get away? You may not be able to recognize violated boundaries in the moment, but the aftermath should be fairly telling. You'll know how tense or unhappy you feel after an interaction.

After that diagnosis, you'll have some time to define exactly what it is about this person that upsets you. Is it something in their character (abrasive, hyperactive, unthinking)? Are they more direct than you're comfortable with? Do they say things to offend or annoy you? Be honest and unsparing with yourself—remember, you don't have to share this information with anybody else.

With all the information you've just gathered—your physical reaction, your mental reaction, and your problem with the person—you've actually come up with a kind of alarm system. If you've ingested all these steps faithfully, the next time you sense any of those things happening, they'll serve as a warning that you need to reexamine or set boundaries.

You'll know when someone's crossed into your personal or emotional space and is putting things in it that aren't your own. You may think of boundaries as a particular kind of violating act, like barging into your apartment and asking for tea, but in reality, whenever you are uncomfortable, chances are a boundary has been crossed. Don't discount your needs here.

Here's an example. Alexa and Elena are sisters. Elena had just introduced her boyfriend Daniel to the family. Daniel started coming to family functions for a few months, and gradually Alexa found herself hanging out with Daniel more often.

But something happened when Alexa was around Daniel. Her stomach got upset when Daniel asked her a question. Her mind got cluttered. Her nerves reacted, and she had the inclination to flee. But she didn't want to tell Daniel off, because she'd possibly tick off Elena and cause a family ruckus.

After Alexa thought about how she reacted around Daniel, she realized he seemed curiously over-interested in other people's private lives—specifically, the romantic parts. Daniel was uncommonly frank in their conversations and sometimes asked personal details that went too far. And he did so in a pleasant way, as if every family in the world has these kinds of conversations freely and openly. He didn't realize his questions were causing tension. But they drove Alexa, a very private person, up the wall. Alexa diagnosed the situation and decided to set some boundaries.

Sure enough, the next time they were together, Daniel started interrogating Alexa about her online dating history. (Alexa had told Elena she'd sworn off online dating for good, which Elena must have told Daniel.) Alexa, very calmly, told Daniel, "Look, I've been giving this a lot of thought, and I just don't feel comfortable discussing my private life in that much detail. I know you don't mean harm and I appreciate your friendliness, but I'm asking you to respect my limits in this matter."

Daniel was taken aback. He had no idea his questions weren't appropriate. He mumbled an apology and walked away. He never asked Alexa anything again. Elena's relationship with Daniel went on for about eight months after the confrontation. While Alexa never cozied up to Daniel in a meaningful way, they did manage a civil and friendly rapport with each other until the breakup, after which Alexa never saw him again.

Alexa's situation worked out fine. It could have been worse: Daniel could have gotten angry, Elena could have gotten upset, and the family could have suffered a big fallout. But whatever the outcome was, Alexa rightfully issued a statement that she had to stand her ground and construct a boundary.

Sometimes there will be fallout from setting boundaries, especially among those who are oblivious as opposed to malicious. But the fallout is almost always worth it—look at the tradeoff Alexa made. Though it may be difficult for you to see in the moment with emotions running high, it's not even close.

How to Set Boundaries

Hopefully you've gotten enough in tune with yourself that you now realize it's time to defend your personal space. Now it's time to do some serious self-investigation and come up with a firm set of boundaries that'll help you curb your people-pleasing addiction. Here are some processes that will help you along.

Determine your core values. Life can be so hectic that you don't have a lot of time for knowing who you are and what you value. Some of us never have that kind of introspection even when we have time to do so. Sometimes, when we try to think about what we believe or value, we may only think about what others tell us to believe or value—our religious beliefs, cultures, or traditions.

It's essential to put all that aside for a little while and concentrate on what *you*, the person, really esteem and what makes up your own, individual personal code. To figure that out, think of things that make you uncomfortable in some way and how they cause you to act. They don't have to be huge, important, or even significant things. They can just be events that happen regularly enough for you to notice them.

For example, Howard couldn't deal with paying an exorbitant amount of money for a parking spot. It doesn't align with his values (or, probably more to the point, what he could afford). But he lived near a big city where he went to professional sporting events, where parking spots regularly cost almost $100 for six hours. No way Howard was dealing with that. Instead, he drove to a park-and-ride and took light rail to the game for $5 round-trip.

Fascinating story, I know. But even this rather slight tale offers a couple ideas about Howard's values:

- He's frugal, at least when it comes to parking spaces.
- He's fine with taking "the long way" if he needs to.
- He supports public transit.

I call those statements "surface values," because they're just a series of indicators as to what Howard's *core* values might be. By doing a little reverse-engineering, we can come up with examples of Howard's potential core values:

- financial responsibility
- patience
- public-mindedness

Try this mental exercise on some of the things *you* do. Take a situation, routine, or event in your life, think about how you act in it, and try to relate them to values you have. You might find some values you weren't completely aware of. Come up with as many examples as you can—eventually, a few core values will keep popping up more than others, and those are probably the ones you *really* believe in.

Here's one important thing to remember: when you're doing this exercise and the event you're analyzing involves your relationship with someone else, make sure you focus on *your* values and what makes *you* comfortable or uneasy. Don't consider what the *other person* might value or frame your values in the context of the relationship. You need to be temporarily selfish in this exercise, because you're trying to figure out what you want. You have permission to be self-centered in this procedure. Once you get a firmer idea of what you stand for, it'll help you become more resolute and curb your tendency to people-please.

Change yourself—and only yourself. While reaffirming your values and getting ready to set boundaries, you might think to yourself, "This situation would be better if my friends/partners/parents/children/coworkers would accept my way of thinking. If everybody could see it my way, there'd be no problem at all."

It's human to want that. When we come across a solution, we want to tell everybody about how we've fixed ourselves: "I was messed up! I'm not messed up anymore! You're still messed up! You need to do exactly what I did!"

Or maybe we just want people to stop being so hard to deal with. We want our partners to stop being so lazy around the house; we want our bosses to stop belittling us; we want our friends to quit being melodramatic. That's human, too.

But go back to what we talked about at the end of the last chapter about breaking habits: "Assume and assert your own *self*-responsibility—things that are completely under your control."

We're not responsible for changing the behaviors of others. Not only that, but trying to change other people almost never works. What you *can* and should change is how you *deal* with other people. You're not going to stop people from attempting to violate your boundaries, but you can change how you deal with these attempts.

This doesn't mean bending over backward to accommodate them (a people-pleaser move). This means changing your personal approach based on those core values we've just discovered and acting in a way that communicates boundaries. It means communicating in a different way with people you're having issues with. It also means standing your emotional ground with people who are being overly aggressive with your personal space.

Let's say someone you're close with is a compulsive over-spender. They're always buying things they don't need. They occasionally ask for loans but always seem to have a lot of stuff or go on vacations more than a broke person should.

You know if this person would just adopt more stringent budgeting practices they'd change their ways. If only they paid closer attention to their bank balance or get better at planning their financial future just like you have. In fact, you're going to march over to this person's apartment with a copy of *Budgeting for Dummies*, and you're going to tell them their lifestyle is a highway to financial insolvency and bankruptcy—right?

Well, no. You're not responsible for this person's problems. You do not have the time to spend fixing them. You have your own things to deal with. But what you *can* do is not give them money anymore. You can only change your behavior to not enable or support other people's behaviors. You are only a part of someone else's mental calculus.

Altering how you deal with others is a much more rewarding exercise than trying to convert people to your way of thinking. Anytime you can work on your own initiative and do something transformative for yourself, it'll be much more effective and fruitful for your own health.

Set the consequences. So what happens after somebody's ignored your limits and happily trespassed into your personal space after you've told them to respect your boundaries?

The answer: whatever you want. Within reason, that is. You're not entitled to start a street fight or hack their computer. But you *are* entitled to stand your emotional ground and defend your personal space. To do that you have to decide what the consequence will be when someone goes past your boundaries. The only thing you're not allowed to do is *nothing*.

For example, let's say there's someone on Facebook who's continually hounding you about a dispute they're having. You've offered warnings to him about pestering you in a public forum, but he keeps doing it. So you decide upon the consequence of un-friending or blocking him from your feed.

This part can be a big, hard step for you emotionally. It's an anxious moment. But it's part of setting your boundaries. This is about *your* needs and yours alone. Those are the needs you have to respect. If someone's crossing that threshold continually despite your admonitions for them to stop, you have to lay down the law for yourself.

You can expect them to react unfavorably, of course. They might call you judgmental, short-sighted, unfair, rash, or irrational. Count on them being that way. Simply consider it part of the process of setting the consequence. But don't let it change your decision.

Another great step to take when setting consequences is writing them down ahead of time. I recommend writing things down for pretty much any situation, but it's especially good to do here. Write down the boundaries you have, the actions others might take that trespass those boundaries, and exactly *what* you will do when they've violated your boundaries. Writing is good for organizing your thoughts and to remind you what you've decided if you need to in the future. It's often difficult to make sound decisions when we're emotional or fearful, so knowing what we've previously decided with a clear mind can help us act.

People-pleasers fear others' disfavor to the point that they allow offenses against them to go unaddressed. Having a firm policy about the consequences of going over your limits help you develop more resolve and self-respect.

More Steps to Setting Boundaries

Nobody else knows what your inner priorities are. Nobody else can tell you how to set up your boundaries. It may sound like a difficult job, but the upshot is that you'll be more prepared to take initiative about reinforcing your values. For anyone trying to get out of a life of people-pleasing, those are critical skills.

Here are more helpful processes on the boundary-setting process.

Get clear and specific on what your boundaries are. You're the one who decides what will work for you and what won't. When you're setting up and explaining your boundaries, you have to be as explicit and direct as you can about them. It's impossible to get someone to respect your boundaries if you're not clear on them yourself. For example, if you don't know that you resent people eating at your dining room table and leaving a mess behind, how will *they*?

When you're establishing these boundaries, think in general terms. Use your core value system to define what you want in more specific areas. Accept that you have a lot of areas to consider when you're setting your personal policies: personal space, personal info, money and possessions, your time and schedule, use of your personal car (that's always a big one), and so forth.

You're allowed to make different boundaries for different people in your life. Not everybody has to follow the same slate of rules and regulations; they can vary according to how close certain people might be to you. It's one thing when a family member or close friend asks if they can borrow your car, but it's quite another when a casual buddy from work or the bar does so. If you feel you need to adjust the boundaries for some and not others, that's your call.

Finally, people might not understand why you've set up certain limitations, rules, or boundaries. That's completely okay. They don't have to. They're your decisions. If other people don't understand that or feel that your rules go against *their* personal emotions or values, it matters not one bit. Don't worry about 'em.

Communicate your boundaries to others in very exact terms. Make sure everybody's very, very clear on what your limits are (especially if they're different for various people). You have an obligation to be clear, candid, and forthright with others about what your boundaries are. You can't assume they'll just guess correctly.

For example, people keep crashing on your sofa. Every weekend, someone you know stays out late and doesn't want to drive back to their home for whatever reason. So they knock on your door, ask if they can crash, you back down, and 15 minutes later your sofa's closed for the night. And there's also a fair chance they'll sneak something from your fridge while you're asleep. It takes personal space away and probably eats a little bit of your time as well.

You probably haven't made it expressly clear that this arrangement no longer works for you. You haven't set this boundary clearly, preferring to passive-aggressively hint that you're annoyed and prefer to not have this happen. So they'll keep doing it because they don't know you have a problem with it. Until you state without equivocation what your boundaries are, folks are going to keep traipsing right through them.

Some people will get it if you just drop a slight hint. For example, take that story about Alexa and Daniel, the guy who asked too-personal questions. Alexa may have expressed her boundaries by simply responding, "Why do you ask?" Many people will pick up on that clue and back off, leaving your boundaries intact.

Others aren't quite as intuitive, and if they keep on not taking the hint, then it's time for you to be explicit and direct with them. This is the tough part. Alexa could have said something like "I don't like to discuss that," "I'm not going to do that," or "Please stop harping on me about this topic." That super-magic word "no" is a direct way to defend your boundaries. Similarly, to defend your couch, you can offer, "This isn't going to work for me anymore" or "This is last time you'll be able to do this without X" or just "This isn't going to happen again."

If someone doesn't understand your set of boundaries and questions you why you have them in place, you are not required to answer them. You don't owe any explanation. You don't have to describe your reasoning or what caused you to make that decision. You don't have to justify a thing. You know yourself, you know what's important to you. You know why you feel the way you do. That is all you need to be concerned about. You don't have to draw a diagram for anybody else. Remember, when communicating your boundaries, "no" is a complete sentence.

Don't let boundary-crossers off the hook. You've figured out your boundaries. You've clearly explained them to others. You've defined what the consequences will be. And yet, someone's still going past your limits. What now?

You have to lay down your personal law and not let the violators off easy. It's time to act.

Implementing your personal boundaries is absolutely necessary when you're trying to establish your limits and assert yourself. That's why *you should only set rules that you are willing to carry out*. Any regulation you set that you're only going to enforce halfway is probably one you should reconsider—you either don't really feel the limit is necessary or you haven't quite worked out all the details. People will take notice and take it as a sign that you aren't very serious about your boundaries—they might as well not exist at that point. This is what is known as a *blurry boundary*, and it's a sign of weakness that people will immediately exploit.

Some folks will resent your setting down limits and dishing out consequences. We'll go a little more into detail about how to contend with more negative outcomes in just a little bit, but for now, know that it will happen.

For example, it would have been easy to simply try and not let your Facebook bully friend bug you. You could have ignored him or found other ways to deal with him. But you know if you allow him to continue to have that access to you, he's only going to keep doing what he does. You've explained yourself, you've defined your limits, and he's ignored them. Hit that "unfriend" button and don't look back.

The people-pleaser has a hard time thinking about what's right for them—let alone standing up for themselves by carrying through on consequences. You'll find that if you back up your boundaries with solid action, there'll be only a small bit of anxiety in the action itself—far less than there would be if you keep letting it fester.

The Three Levels of Personal Boundaries

You now know how to define your personal boundaries, explain them, and enforce them. And you also know that boundary rules can be different according to who you're dealing with. Now let's discuss what actually happens when people cross over into your personal space, whether they're invited or not.

When you're involved in an interaction with someone, there are basically three levels that depict how deeply you're protecting your boundaries. Simply put, there's too strong, too weak, and just right.

Healthy. The goal is to maintain your boundaries in a balanced manner. A healthy boundary will reinforce your character, moderate your emotional reactions, and help you be generous in a meaningful way.

When you have healthy boundaries, you have a healthy respect for yourself, your feelings, and your viewpoint. You don't sell out your core values so others can take advantage of them. You exchange and reveal personal information in a suitable and proper way. You're also able to handle it when people say no to you.

Rigid. You can also be extra-firm when setting your boundaries and turn yourself into an impenetrable fortress. But there are serious drawbacks to this approach. You're likely to have few if any intimate or close relationships with anyone. You'll appear distant and removed to other people, possibly completely isolated. You'll be reticent to ask anyone else for assistance, and you'll keep yourself away from vulnerable situations so you don't have to deal with rejection.

The rigid boundary-setter does everything possible to avoid being exposed, weak, or too available because they don't want to get hurt by anybody else. But in doing so, they still get hurt—by themselves.

Porous. Someone with very thin boundaries tends to let a lot of people and forces into their life to basically act out their will. When you keep porous boundaries, you tend to give out too much personal information or get far too involved in the problems of other people. "No" is a word you have an extremely difficult time saying. You open yourself up to discourteous and abusive people—in fact, you practically invite and permit people to take advantage of your goodwill.

The porous boundary-setter is far too trusting and unreserved about other people. They get exploited on a regular basis, even by people with no intentions to exploit them. They're often disappointed and can become bitter about their existence even as they still over-share themselves. This is another way of describing blurry boundaries.

Looking over this information, you're probably inclined to believe that the healthy level is the one you should shoot for 100% of the time. That's not a terrible place to start. But you *will* find that you might need to adjust in either direction depending on certain factors.

For example, if you have a good relationship with your family, most likely you'd be a little more porous to them. If you're in a working relationship with someone you mistrust, you'd probably nudge yourself toward the rigid policy.

You have the freedom to decide how far you'll bend or expand your boundaries in a given situation. But there are very few, if any, situations where it's a good idea to be full-on rigid or porous. Thick-bordered people are hard to reach, are very defensive, and practically walk around in full body armor. Thin-bordered ones are overly open and frequently naïve—they're easy to get close to, but their naked sincerity can let bad forces in.

Also, consider that different world cultures have differing standards of emotional display and behaviors—some cultures are very open and demonstrative with affections; others are more reserved and professional. This can make world travel hilarious.

The main thing to consider when you're setting your boundaries, as I've said several times, is that you're the one in charge. You have to trust in yourself and believe what you need, want, and cherish is right. And you have to know that your feelings are equally as important as anyone else's.

Setting Boundaries in the Middle of a Situation

It's always great to have everything planned out in advance. But situations will come up in which you'll find your boundaries being penetrated, and you'll have to make situational, on-the-fly adjustments to keep yourself intact and healthy. Circumstances happen that you're not instinctively prepared for, and when they do, you'll need to react in a way that keeps your boundaries in place.

Your response should always send a clear message. But if you're trying to get over your people-pleasing habit, it may be easier to be subtle and strong. After all, you're used to appeasing everyone, so turning that mode off and being tough and decisive might not be possible.

For demonstration purposes, here are a few topics and emotions that may arise suddenly in an unforeseen situation. I'll give you two possible responses for each: one that's subtle and considerate, in the hopes that hints will be picked up, and another that's more direct and to the point after it becomes clear that force is needed. Of course, the phrasing here can be applied to many circumstances.

Money. Everyone needs to be paid, but there might be a couple of friends or associates who keep needing assistance. You can't be expected to keep giving out money you've earned or is rightfully yours to someone who can't respect your limits.

- Subtle: "I'm sorry about the situation you're in. I just have limited resources right now and don't have the room to lend money at the moment."

- Direct: "I can't keep lending you money. I have to use it for my own needs and upkeep. You need to find a way to take care of yourself and get money on your own."

Extra commitments. Often, we find ourselves giving too much of our time away, and it's especially troublesome when we're maxing out our energies in efforts we genuinely care about. But instead of over-promising on something, defend and guard the time you need to pay attention to other aspects of your life.

- Subtle: "I'm very sympathetic to your cause, but although I care about it myself, I'm afraid my bandwidth is maxed out. I'd be happy to talk about it once I get more time."

- Direct: "I can't help right now. I just don't have the time."

Un-constructive criticism. Judgment, character assassination, and harsh jokes about your appearance or manner are almost never okay, but they can be tricky to defend after you've been shocked and hurt. But it's vital to stand up for yourself as soon as you can.

- Subtle: "I realize you may have been making a joke or weren't being serious, but I felt hurt at the comments you made. It's a sensitive issue with me. I hope you understand."

- Direct: "I don't appreciate your remarks. I'm not going to be part of this conversation if you keep on making them."

Anger. Disagreements happen, but when emotions get out of hand, it's unfortunately easy for someone to break protocol and become hostile and abusive. It's important to be calm but strong about taking down the temperature.

- Subtle: "I need you to try and be less angry. You're making it difficult to communicate. The only way we're going to fix this situation is by being reasonable. Could you try to use a more measured tone?"

- Direct: "Don't scream at me. Would you tolerate it yourself? I'm leaving the room. When you've calmed yourself down and won't threaten me, we might be able to resume this discussion."

Buying time. There might be a time when someone says they urgently need you to make an instant decision and do something immediately. As the business cliché goes, their emergency is not your priority. Stand firm on your schedule.

- Subtle: "I understand what you're saying. I just need some time to think about what the best way would be to go forward. I realize you feel this is urgent, but can I get back to you on this? That would be helpful."

- Direct: "I'm not going to force myself to make a quick decision without giving it more thought. I need time to

> consider it further. If you can't wait another minute for my answer, then the answer is no."

Knowing how to adjust and react in the middle of an unexpected boundary-crossing incident makes it easier to resist sudden urges to people-please.

Prepare for the Aftermath

Now for the fun part! When you finally take the personal initiative to respect yourself and set and defend your boundaries, it may bend a few people out of shape. They won't be happy. They'll be upset and maybe sad. A few of them might be really pissed off. But staying firm to your boundaries will actually *help* your relationships and alliances over the long haul.

If someone else's response makes you let down your boundaries, you're going to feel irritated with them as time goes on. You can't let yourself be deterred by them. You need a situation where your friends, relations, and associates truly esteem you for who you are and will respect your limits—even if they feel a little let down or unhappy with your decision at first.

Like any good business plan, you have to account for a certain measure of risk to make your boundary settings more likely to succeed. In this case, you have to allow for—in fact, fully anticipate—that someone might be angry when you set your boundaries.

You therefore need to steel your resolve with someone who might be unreasonably mad with you. You can't accept their bullying or their attempts to break your limits. You can't let them continue to exploit your sympathy or helpfulness or show disdain for the boundaries that are completely your right to establish.

If you allow an angry person to weaken your determination because they scare you, your situation will not improve. Realize this as quickly as you can. By withdrawing your request that they respect your limits, you'll only get more depressed and displeased. In time, that turns into full-on acrimony and hatred.

On the other hand, if you stand firm in the face of someone's indignation with you, the discomfort will only be temporary. They may continue to feel resentful for a bit, but you'll at least know that you've stood your ground and defended what's important to you. At least *you* will eventually feel confident that you've made the right choice. Chances are their anger will die down as well, and you'll still have a relationship you can build back up again.

Whatever's making them so angry isn't your problem—it's *theirs*. Once again, you're responsible only for your own actions and deeds. *They* are responsible for *their own* reactions. If you sustain an even temperament and hold firm to your convictions about boundaries, maybe they'll finally learn they need to respect others more often.

Don't take an angry person's bait. If their rage is starting to careen out of control, keep yourself calm. Don't let them dictate the hostile tone of the exchange just because they're infuriated. This is one of those rare situations where remaining idle is a sign of strength. Let them storm their head off, and quietly go about your business.

Another thing people-pleasers often do in the presence of an angry person is to immediately try and make them feel better and get back in their good graces. They frequently do this without thinking. But you should resist the urge to make it all better as well, because you'll still be ceding your personal power to someone who's just going to consume it.

When dealing with the fire and fury of someone who's angry with your decisions, including those in which you establish your boundaries, the solution is marvelously simple: do nothing. It's not always easy, but it's almost always the best way.

To get out of people-pleasing mode, one needs to understand the importance of forming boundaries, determine what their personal ones are, keep guard over them, and aggressively defend them when they're being transgressed. Harnessing that strength of character will remind you of your value and beliefs—and will take you out of the subservient position of trying to satisfy everyone.

Takeaways:

- Strong and clear boundaries will be one of your best defenses against people-pleasing and the people that would have you do so. However, they can't exist solely in your head, and they can't be so flexible that people see no reason to abide by them. Thus, you must communicate them clearly and enforce them without exception.

- First, you need to define your boundaries by exploring what your core and surface values are. This is how you know what you should protect and what you can let go of. Communicate them to others.

- The other major aspect is setting consequences and then enforcing them. This is what happens when someone attempts to violate your boundaries after you've communicated them. This is can be whatever you want; the only thing it cannot be is *nothing*. Failure to do so will create porous boundaries, which are as good as no boundaries at all. However, they also cannot be too rigid.

- Unfortunately, you will almost always have some sort of negative reaction to your boundaries. This is something you have to prepare for, but it will be difficult nonetheless. People don't like getting told no, but that reflects on them, not you as a person.

Chapter 6: How to Say No

Learning to say no can be the ultimate assertive skill a person can possess. Most of us aim to please, and as we've learned throughout this book, it's not necessarily our fault. It may not even be a conscious decision to be unable to say no.

Somewhere in our lives, we've discovered that that we bring negativity and possible confrontation or disappointment into an interaction. Or we don't set proper and rigid boundaries. Or any of the multitude of reasons we've talked about related to a lack of assertiveness in this book. The end result of saying yes when you want to say no is the same no matter what, and that's what this chapter aims to address. You already know what you need to do, and you might even understand your psychological holdups.

That doesn't magically make saying no easy and remove the inherent tension. In fact, you will probably never get 100% accustomed to the tension, but at the very least, you can learn specific phrases and tactics to say no that will help you communicate your message more gracefully and smoothly.

"I Can't" vs. "I Don't"

You might be surprised to know that how we talk to ourselves can impact our ability to say no. *The Journal of Consumer Research* published a study in which 120 students were divided into two groups: the "I can't" group and the "I don't" group. One group was told that each time they were faced with temptation they were to tell themselves, "I can't do X." For example, when tempted with chocolate, they were to say, "I can't eat chocolate." The other group, the "I don't" group, was instructed to say, "I don't do X" or, in the case of chocolate, "I don't eat chocolate."

The results of this study showed the major impact that just a slight difference in vocabulary can make on our ability to say no, to resist temptation, and to motivate goal-directed behavior. The "I don't" group was overwhelming more successful in its ability to say no.

If you tell yourself "I can't," you're simply reminding yourself of the limitations you've set for yourself. You're creating a feedback loop in your brain that tells you that you can't do something that you would normally want to do. "I can't" becomes an exercise in self-discipline, which is not something you want to constantly depend on.

On the other hand, when you tell yourself "I don't," you're creating a feedback loop that reminds you of your power and control of the situation. You've given yourself a line in the sand that takes the situation out of your hands. Your choice was premade to say no and thus you can stick to it more easily. By simply changing one word when we talk to ourselves, we can change our behavior. When people hear "don't," it's more of a hard boundary, whereas "can't" typically implies an open-ended answer that encourages people to try to persuade and coax you.

For example, consider a situation in which someone on a diet is offered a calorie-loaded dessert. If they say "I can't," they are reminding themselves of the limitations created by their diet. They have thought about it and made an active decision to say no. If they instead say "I don't" when offered the same dessert, they'll be taking control of the situation and only have to stick to their premade decision. They'll be reminding themselves that they don't eat foods that are full of calories.

The "I don't" mantra can be an invaluable tool in our daily lives. In saying "I don't let my friends talk me into things I don't want to do" or "I don't eat between meals," we make it a lot easier to say no or resist temptation. We also empower ourselves and make it much easier to achieve our goals and objectives. We are talking both to ourselves and the requesters.

You've got a policy and you're sticking it!

Rejecting Categories

In learning to say no, the same "I don't" principle applies to someone who gets repeated requests for favors or obligations. Instead of reviewing each request separately, you might consider rejecting the entire category.

In other words, instead of reviewing each request and making an "I can" or an "I can't" decision, you'll find that it's much more empowering to reject all requests that are in a certain category, such as "Sorry, I don't do those types of meetings anymore."

This approach will take all of the decision-making out of requests from other people and you'll find that it's much easier to say no to these requests. Yes, you can make exceptions to requests when it's something you really want to do or really need to do, but you'll find that it will be much easier to opt into a request than it is to opt out. Just like with saying "I don't" as opposed to "I can't," refusing an entire category is a boundary that most people will accept. If they sense you make exceptions frequently, they will attempt to persuade you to let them be yet another one.

As an example, our old friend Jack is a well-known author whose crime novels have sold hundreds of thousands of copies. As a result, he gets numerous requests from groups who invite him to attend their meetings and discuss these books. Inundated with requests from groups as small as five or six people and as large as 200 people, Jack has established his own criteria for speaking to groups about his books. He won't speak to any groups of less than 20 and he won't make any group presentations in the months of May through August, as those are the months he wants to use to write his next book and those are also months when his kids are out of school and he wants to make sure he spends time with them then.

In forming his own restrictive criteria to filter guest speaking requests, Jack finds it much easier to say no to many of the numerous requests he receives. He already knows what his rules are, and it's easier to abide to a blanket rule than decide who deserves to be an exception.

Once again, if it's difficult for you to say no, you should resolve to start rejecting categories. Resolve to say no whenever someone asks you for a favor. Automatically reject the request, categorically. Then, if it is something you really want to do, you can always opt in and say yes. But no should be your preferred response.

If you have people in your life that make repeated requests, it might be better to preempt their request. "I know you're moving at the end of the month. If you need help moving, I'll have to take a raincheck this time around. My wife and I agreed that we should make an effort to spend more time with the kids."

The Relational Account

The problem with no is that it's negative. Well—I suppose that's obvious, isn't it? Despite its power when used correctly, no isn't an easy thing for people to say, especially for someone caught up in people-pleasing. No matter your reasons for saying no, the other party will probably experience it as rejection.

Saying no directly—even if you're polite and your reasons are legitimate—can affect how others perceive you. They might think you're frigid, standoffish, or ungenerous. Whether any of those characteristics are fair or not, they demonstrate how much power the word "no" wields.

How do we stand our ground when there's far too much on our plate to take care of new requests? Wharton professor and writer Adam Grant came upon the idea of relational account—or, as he puts it, "If I helped you, I'd be letting others down."

The relational account simply involves making mention of your responsibilities and obligations to another person when you turn the asker down.

For example, if a friend asks you to housesit their home for an extended period of time they'll be away, you could say, "I just have too many responsibilities right now—my partner and I are remodeling our home so it'll be easier for our kids. I'm needed on that front right now. You need someone who's going to be able to give it full attention."

If someone is asking you to cover for them at work, you could say, "I'm working on a very involved project that's keeping me from taking part in a lot of things I'm interested in, unfortunately. I just don't have the capacity for all the things I'd like to do."

The relational account method works because it infers that you're actually a positive, caring person. The reason you can't help out is that you're over-booked or that there's someone else depending on you. This reduces the requester's feeling of rejection and takes away the chance that you'll be stigmatized as a crank or a grouch just because you said no.

This is especially handy for the recovering people-pleaser, as it helps maintain whatever positive reputation they might have. You won't go from a feckless helper to a sharp denier overnight.

"Yes. What Should I De-Prioritize?"

In situations when you've got too much on your plate, someone might make a request that would crowd your schedule even more. If agreeing to their request is going to imperil your productivity, you absolutely have to deny them in some way, whether in work, in public, or at home. But it can still be very hard to say no, especially to people with authority like a boss or those we have strong feelings for and don't want to let down.

For these situations, another way of saying no is by saying yes—with a catch. Agree to do what they ask of you but *also* ask them which of your many other responsibilities should you cease working on to make room for their request.

The de-prioritizing angle is especially good for work situations in which you're answering to someone higher up than you: "Sure, I'll be happy to help you go through our budget for next year. What other job can I put aside for now so I can focus on that? Should I put the marketing presentation or the archive project on the back-burner for now?"

But it's effective in personal situations as well. "I'd be happy to help you move this weekend, but I'd have to cancel either my visit with my mom or my kid's ballet recital. What would you do?" "I can help you with painting the living room. Should I de-prioritizing cleaning up the garage or working on the vegetable garden?"

This approach works for many reasons. Your "yes" response sends a positive message and suggests a spirit of willingness. In asking your requestor to pick what items to pass over for now, you're giving the asker the appearance of having an option (when, in actuality, it's *you* that's making the choice). Perhaps most importantly, it is a subtle way to say, "I've got too much on my plate right now." It draws attention that they have asked for too much and that you are not intending to satisfy their every whim.

You're also establishing yourself as a methodical schedule-setter, because you have way too much going on—but you keep it organized and under control. Finally, you're setting a boundary for yourself in the politest way possible. Especially if you're trying to break out of people-pleasing mode, those are crucial steps to take.

Plant Seeds by Preemptively Saying No

I'm sure you know a couple people who nurse a constant habit of asking for things. You can almost sense their need the minute they walk into the room. You know at some point—probably several—they're going to make a request of you that you'll have to deny.

In those cases, there's a very subtle trick that you can use to refuse them. The reason it's tricky is because you use it in a situation when they're *not* asking you for anything. It's something you do in a normal conversation or meeting.

When you're talking with the person you know is going to hit you up at some point, talk about everything going on in your life that will require that you say no to someone in the near (or even distant) future. This is just like the relational account, except you're using it before you get asked to do anything.

Talk about how busy you are and all the things you do. Explain how you're strapped for resources like money or manpower. Tell them all the reasons that you have to say no to *other* people in your life at the moment, besides them.

For example, if you're with a friend who you think might ask to crash at your house for an extended period of time, you can say, "My house is getting really cramped—there's no room for me to have any personal space, it seems. I'm always crowded out. It's so jam-packed in there I can't even have people over for a visit."

If you're anticipating that someone at work will ask you to take on new responsibilities (especially if you know your company's reorganizing in advance), you can say, "I can't believe how busy I've been lately. There are so many new things I have to account for that I'm still working them into my daily schedule. I don't know how I keep up with them all."

This works because it establishes your grounds for saying no for the foreseeable future. You've produced the perception that you have a very full life and schedule that doesn't leave you a lot of room to take on or do something new. And when the serial asker *does* make their request, you can remind them that you've already mentioned why you have to say no: "Like I told you the other day, I've got a million things on my plate right now."

The ultimate goal in the preemptive denial is, of course, that people will stop requesting things from you. They'll know ahead of time you're probably not going to be able to help them. This is an ex-people-pleaser's dream scenario.

You could become so skillful at saying no in these situations that you'll be able to issue a preemptive denial *way* before the asker even knows they're going to ask. That guy who you think is going to ask you to join his expensive fantasy football league? You can just say something like, "I'm so broke. I'm going to have to work so much that I don't think I'm going to be following football this year."

Keep It Simple

The best way to say no is to be simple and straightforward. There are no tricks around how to do it; it's just the inherent discomfort and tension of the act.

If you've been passive for a long time, people are going to be surprised when you say no. And if you're dealing with someone who has an alpha personality, they will almost surely try to get you to change your decision. Heck, your lack of assertiveness might by why they hang around you in the first place, and it's tough to change that relationship dynamic once it's been set. Expect pushback and shock when you change the dynamic.

The worst thing you can do in such a predicament is revise your decision. If you do, you'll know that you'll have to face the same predicament with the same person whenever they have future requests. And they'll know that your no is negotiable. Become a broken record. Each time they ask, answer with a quick and simple no, leaving no room for negotiation. If you appear to have wiggle room, you'll just be encouraging people to continue to persuade you.

Resist the moment. The toughest time in saying no usually occurs right after you do so. It's then when you want to offer help, keep talking, or do anything to reduce the tension that your no has created. This is usually the time when you start wavering: "Well, if you really need my help, I guess I could..." "I'd rather not, but..." Resist the temptation and stay silent, because your assertiveness is often lost in that moment.

When saying no, remember that you don't need to make excuses. You can say you're busy, it's not in your wheelhouse, or whatever your reason is, but that's it. Leave it at that. If you still feel the need to add a "because" at the end of your sentence, keep it short and simple and don't elaborate on the details. The more details you give, the more fodder you give people to pick at. For instance, if you say no to helping a friend move because you need to walk your cat in the morning, you create an avenue for people to dispute that you need to walk a cat at all.

Don't hem and haw your way through a lame explanation on why you said no. Don't feel compelled to share an alternative or something that can make up for your no. It's okay to just say no. No further explanation is needed. Overall, remember that no can be a complete sentence.

Create hoops. If you can't just say no or if you can't say no immediately, another option is to defer the decision or punt it into the future. Tell them you'll think about it and, if applicable, ask them to do something to prepare you for it. In other words, put the burden back on them by requesting something to help you consider their request. Confused?

Let's take Jonathan, who is very smart and mentors companies. He is asked for coffee all the time from people who would like to "pick his brain" and otherwise soak up information from him like a sponge. As you can imagine, he doesn't have time for everyone that asks him. He has to say no quite frequently, but he's devised a way around it. He creates a hoop for them to jump through before he agrees to anything further. When someone asks him for coffee, he will ask them to send, via email, an agenda or plan of what they want to discuss and why. He doesn't hear from 99% of the people again.

As you can see from Jonathan's case, it becomes very clear who just wants to use you for something without being willing to contribute in any way or make it easy for you. When someone asks you for something, create a condition for them to fulfill in order for you to consider their request. It will buy you time and space, and most people will never get back to you because they would have to put in the work!

Another related way to say no is something to the effect of "I'm not sure right now, but can you follow up with me?" It has the same effect of shifting the burden onto someone else, and we already know, of course, that the best-case scenario from shifting the burden onto someone else is that they just leave you alone out of laziness or they forget. You can also use the variety of "I can't right now, but maybe when my circumstances change."

Bait and switch. Another option, if you're having a tough time saying no, will be to offer a bait and switch yes: “I can’t do that, but I can do this.”

“I can’t spend all day helping you move to another apartment, but I can give you two hours.”
“I can’t go out with you this weekend, but I promise that I’ll make some time to do that within the next month.”
“I can’t serve on the board, but I’ll be willing to consult on an ad-hoc basis whenever I have time.”

What you’re doing here is saying no to the request and offering a smaller consolation prize that may or may not be refused. It may be a legitimate alternative as something you are willing to do, but it doesn’t have to be.

Your no is disguised because you appear to be still open and willing, at least on the surface. If you offer something relatively small, people will likely refuse and tell you not to bother with it. Even better is if you don’t provide specific detail and leave it as open-ended as possible. In most cases, the bait and switch will result in freedom from an ask or obligation. This tactic alleviates most of the tension because you are saying yes to something, just not what is specifically being asked.

Keep it nonpersonal. Many times when we say no, it feels terrible because we know how we'd feel when we get rejected. We might take it personally and ruminate on how much someone doesn't care about us or perhaps how the symbolic value is lacking. Therefore, it's important to keep your no as nonpersonal as possible and as focused on the specific situation at hand as possible.

In essence, you are rejecting the person because of the situation and circumstances, not because of the person themselves. Some people have difficulty separating the two, but the former is much, much easier to both speak and hear.

For instance, you are invited to a friend's party only to learn that your ex, with whom you had a particularly nasty split, will be there. Your friend is giving you grief about passing it up, but in reality, it's not about your friend: it's about the situation and being in an enclosed area with someone who makes you nauseous. In this case, you would emphasize that you aren't saying no to spending time with your friend, which is what they might perceive, but instead saying no to being in your ex's presence.

A little bit of regret always helps—for instance, "I'd really love to and I was really looking forward to hanging out with you, but I can't!" When people feel validated and not rejected, they'll accept a no far more easily. Just be sure to focus on the specific circumstances and how they won't work for you.

Pass the buck. Here, you aren't saying no as much as "Yes, but..." Allow me to explain. Passing the buck means passing the responsibility onto someone else who is not you.

It's when you suggest that someone else would be a much better, more qualified fit than you, and thus, you should bow out. You wouldn't do the requester justice, but you can still help them solve their problem by finding someone who will. The requester won't necessarily hear a no, which is the most important part.

For instance, if you are asking someone to drive you to the airport, you might say, "No, I'm a terrible driver and driving on the highways make me feel anxious, but Ted is a great driver and might be free that day!" You've successfully passed the buck to Ted by making yourself pale in comparison to how Ted might solve the issue.

People ask you for things because they want to solve a problem they have. If you make yourself seem like a terrible solution, but at the same time can point them in the direction of a real solution, you've avoided a duty.

Saying no is a valuable skill. In learning to say no, you'll be able to take control of your life and your time. In learning to say no, you'll empower yourself to avoid the things you don't want to do. In learning to say no properly, you'll be able to avoid tension, confrontation, and ruffled feathers. A life devoid of no is one that is not your own; it is one that is lived for other people.

Like any skill, the ability to say no is often an acquired talent. You, too, can learn how to say no. It may take some time and some practice, but when you become proficient at saying no, you'll wonder what to do with all the free time you now possess.

As mentioned before, you're going to face at least a little repercussion for standing your ground. That's going to happen when you start saying no as well, even if you use some of the more creative ways we've talked about in this chapter.

The people you used to automatically please might be unreasonably offended because they'll no longer have regular access to you. They've been accustomed to just expecting things from you and your doing them without protest. That's not the case anymore because you've altered that relationship, so you can expect some initial blowback.

But in time—just like when you set your boundaries—that anger will recede and hopefully evolve into respect. You'll be seen as someone who is responsible, organized, and deliberate, not just an over-willing people-pleaser.

Takeaways:

- Saying no is one of the toughest situations in everyday life because it is a mini confrontation every single time. But there are many ways to make this part of life smoother and less tense.
- Start saying "I don't" versus "I can't" because the former implies a policy, whereas the latter implies something to be negotiated. Likewise, get into the habit of saying no to specific and broad categories because that also implies a policy that you don't make exceptions for.
- There are countless ways to say no. You already know a few, including the simplest way: "no" as a complete

sentence. Understand that people will react strongly to you if you have a history of people-pleasing and being a doormat.

- Other methods of saying no include planting preemptive seeds, emphasizing how you are tied to other people and can't act independently, referencing the fact that you can't do everything at once, resisting the moment where you want to insert an addendum or caveat, creating hoops for people to jump through and themselves say yes to, baiting and switching with related or unrelated tasks, keeping it nonpersonal and focused on the specific circumstance, and passing the buck to someone who appears to be able to solve the problem at hand much better than you.

Cheat Sheet

Chapter 1: The Fatal Need to Please

- The need to please others may appear to be generous and selfless, but it is one of the most selfish ways of behavior. People-pleasing is borne out of fear, insecurity, and a need for approval. It is predicated on the sad belief that you are not enough and that you thus need to increase your value by catering to people's needs and desires.

- The origins of people-pleasing instincts can come from a variety of sources, but the dynamic is always the same. You sought approval, were denied, and had to prove yourself in another way. You were gradually taught through experience that you received better outcomes when you served and placated people, so that became your natural state of being.

- This compulsion is further compounded by the spotlight effect, in which we have the distorted belief that everyone is constantly watching us and picking us apart. This is detrimental for "normal" people, but it's even worse for people-pleasers because it drives takes their insecurity to new levels, which causes a host of detrimental behaviors.

- Make no mistake about it; people-pleasing is harmful. You may get the approval you seek on a short-term basis, but it will be fleeting and fake. Then you will have to deal with the consequences—for instance, repression and suppression leaking out in passive-aggressive behavior, finally exploding like a volcano, or generally compromised happiness and health because of the overwhelming number of tasks you give yourself. Finally, you might end up with skewed relationships because you are putting yourself in a subordinate role and constantly putting on a face.

Chapter 2: The Origins and Causes of People-Pleasing

- There are many causes of people-pleasing behavior, and they start with the beliefs we hold about ourselves in relation to others. Simply put, we are not the same; we are lower or inferior in some way. This sets up interpersonal dynamics that enable people-pleasing and in fact reward it. I've divided it into four main categories that cause these beliefs.
- First is a skewed definition of relationships and how serving others should be your first priority, to the detriment of yourself. If you possess this belief, you will be wracked with guilt if you attempt to act against it.
- Second is a sense of low self-worth. If you don't feel that you are equal to others or that others will accept you for you, then it becomes clear that your only chance of acceptance is to bend over backward and serve people's whims.
- Third, we have been taught from infancy that generosity and kindness are

admirable traits. Some of us take this too far and equate prioritizing oneself to be selfish and negative.

- Finally, many people-pleasers simply fear confrontation. They hate the tension and discomfort and will go to extreme lengths to avoid it. They don't want to make waves and are solely focused on flying under the radar.

Chapter 3: Reprogram Your Beliefs

- A lifetime of people-pleasing will lead to some deeply ingrained beliefs that require reprogramming. A staple of changing beliefs is cognitive behavioral therapy, which is, in short, a way to combat skewed beliefs with thoughtfulness and pointing out negative patterns. The easy way to think about this is through BLUE—"B" stands for blaming myself, "L" is looking for bad news, "U" means unhappy guessing, and "E" represents exaggeratedly negative thoughts. We can apply these to the four major causes of people-pleasing behavior from the previous chapter.

- You must be more selfish. Often, we have the belief that selfishness is always bad and never good. The reality is that you must be selfish, even if you want to serve others, because only then can you operate at full capacity. Selfishness does not mean throwing others under the bus, and it simply means prioritizing your body and mind.
- You must accept and love yourself. Your relationship with yourself determines your relationship with everyone else, so you should be more compassionate to yourself and understand that acceptance is a choice—typically made more difficult by impossible standards and expectations you place on yourself.
- You must believe that assertiveness is not inherently bad and does not equal aggressiveness. Consider what you would do in other people's shoes and be creative in finding ways that both people win in a situation.
- You must accept and grow more comfortable with confrontation. A good method to get over a fear of confrontation is to use exposure

therapy. Specifically, create a fear hierarchy for yourself as related to confrontation. This will help you grow used to the tension and also show that you nothing ill will occur if you face your fears.

Chapter 4: Change Your Habits

- Unfortunately, over time, please-pleasing behaviors tend to become solidified as habits—automatic responses to the world. We may intend something different, but if our first and second instincts are to please, we are not improving at being assertive. Therefore, it becomes necessary to change a few of these unconscious habits to break your detrimental patterns.
- Build self-awareness of why you are engaging in people-pleasing behaviors and you will be able to realize that you aren't doing it out of free will or generosity. This can be as easy as asking yourself "why" five times in a row to try

to understand what's behind your actions.

- Build autonomy and become freer from the opinions and thoughts of others. Value your own opinions and thoughts, and don't automatically subordinate yourself to others.

- Do less and stop creating one-sided relationships. You've conditioned people to rely on you, and to reverse this, you must give them the space to act for themselves.

- Let go of your past. It informs who you are, but you are not your experiences and memories. Try to realize when you are acting out of the past or out of your own free will.

- Remain strong under pressure. When you stop people-pleasing, you will face some angry reactions. It's not necessarily their fault because you have conditioned their expectations. But this is where you must not fold under pressure, like you previously would have. It only takes five seconds of extreme willpower, and it gets easier every time thereafter.

- Stop taking responsibility for other people's emotions and happiness. Everyone is responsible for their own emotions and happiness. You do not need to be someone's emotional guardian, especially if it is harmful to you.

Chapter 5: Set Your Boundaries

- Strong and clear boundaries will be one of your best defenses against people-pleasing and the people that would have you do so. However, they can't exist solely in your head, and they can't be so flexible that people see no reason to abide by them. Thus, you must communicate them clearly and enforce them without exception.

- First, you need to define your boundaries by exploring what your core and surface values are. This is how you know what you should protect and what you can let go of. Communicate them to others.

- The other major aspect is setting consequences and then enforcing them. This is what happens when someone attempts to violate your boundaries after you've communicated them. This is can be whatever you want; the only thing it cannot be is *nothing*. Failure to do so will create porous boundaries, which are as good as no boundaries at all. However, they also cannot be too rigid.

- Unfortunately, you will almost always have some sort of negative reaction to your boundaries. This is something you have to prepare for, but it will be difficult nonetheless. People don't like getting told no, but that reflects on them, not you as a person.

Chapter 6: How to Say No

- Saying no is one of the toughest situations in everyday life because it is a mini confrontation every single time.

But there are many ways to make this part of life smoother and less tense.

- Start saying "I don't" versus "I can't" because the former implies a policy, whereas the latter implies something to be negotiated. Likewise, get into the habit of saying no to specific and broad categories because that also implies a policy that you don't make exceptions for.
- There are countless ways to say no. You already know a few, including the simplest way: "no" as a complete sentence. Understand that people will react strongly to you if you have a history of people-pleasing and being a doormat.
- Other methods of saying no include planting preemptive seeds, emphasizing how you are tied to other people and can't act independently, referencing the fact that you can't do everything at once, resisting the moment where you want to insert an addendum or caveat, creating hoops for people to jump through and themselves say yes to, baiting and switching with related or unrelated

tasks, keeping it nonpersonal and focused on the specific circumstance, and passing the buck to someone who appears to be able to solve the problem at hand much better than you.

Made in the USA
Las Vegas, NV
07 March 2023

68694370R00129